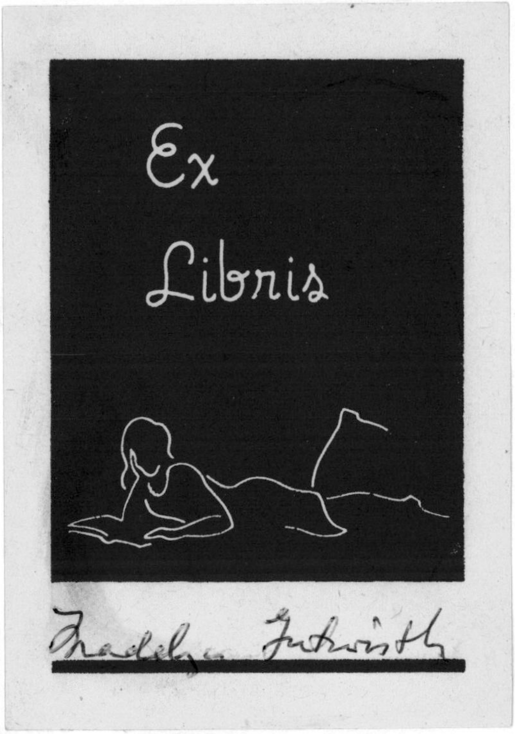
Ex
Libris

MEN AND WOMEN
FEMINISM AND ANTI-FEMINISM TODAY

MEN AND WOMEN
Feminism and Anti-Feminism Today

by

KENNETH HUDSON

DAVID & CHARLES : NEWTON ABBOT

7153 4298 3

Printed in Great Britain by
Bristol Typesetting Co. Ltd., Barton Manor, Bristol BS2 0RN
for David & Charles (Holdings) Limited
South Devon House Railway Station
Newton Abbot Devon

Contents

The case of women is now the only case in which to rebel against established rules is still looked upon with the same eyes as was formerly a subject's claim to the right of rebelling against his king.

John Stuart Mill: *The Subjection of Women* (1869)

Introduction

There is no shortage of information about the history of the feminist movement in Britain. The library of the Fawcett Society, which is wholly devoted to the subject, contains 20,000 books and a very large collection of pamphlets, letters, cuttings, posters, prints and photographs. The most dramatic and best publicised aspect of the movement, women's struggle to get the vote, has been much described and analysed in many books. The author of one of the best of them, Roger Fulford, has accurately observed that the enjoyment and information they provide frequently has to be 'disengaged from a certain masculine condescension from the one sex and an almost apostolic fervour from the other'.[1] The suffragettes got what they wanted, and for more than forty years now women have been able to vote on the same terms as men. The same period has seen considerable improvements in the legal position of women.

Yet, once one moves away from definite and limited reforms, it is obvious that change has come much more slowly. This is particularly true of the opportunities provided, or not provided, for women who want to work outside their homes, in investment and the handling of money, in public work and in what Vera Brittain has called 'the vast inchoate sphere of manners and morals'.[2] Here, the speed of change has been governed by tradition, prejudice and superstition, as well as by women's own uncertainty as to the kind of satisfaction they really want from life.

Notes to this chapter are on page 167

In many respects, Britain in the 1960s can be justly regarded as a paradise by women who live in other European countries. In the Soviet Union, usually thought of as a country where women suffer no legal or employment disadvantages, there is no such thing as part-time work for them. They must either work seven hours a day, five and a half days a week, or not at all. Faced with this situation, large numbers of women refuse to take employment and, to meet a labour shortage in certain types of factory work, the first stirrings have been heard of a movement to bring the Soviet Union into line with the West and to encourage part-time work as socially useful, both to the state and to women. In France, although the sale and use of contraceptives is not illegal, it is a crime punishable by imprisonment to advertise birth-control advice in any way.[3] One result of this has inevitably been a large number of abortions. A careful investigation carried out by Katia Kaupp in 1964-5 showed that in France there were as many abortions as births.[4] In Paris, births were about 95,000 a year and abortions 150,000. In a small village near Chartres a forty-four-year-old woman had recently died of exhaustion after the birth of her twenty-third child; nobody had ever told her about any form of birth-control.

French women suffer from other forms of inferior status, which would undoubtedly cause great indignation in Britain.[5] By French law, the husband alone possesses what are called 'paternal powers'. This means that all dealings with the authorities, particularly where children are concerned, such as those relating to schools, medical care, or applications for scholarships, have to be made through the husband, although in actual practice it is the mother who almost invariably handles such matters. A French woman finds herself in a most difficult situation if her husband has become insane, since the almost unbelievable principle accepted in French law is that 'a sane woman does not equal a husband who has gone mad'. Even when insane, the husband retains his paternal powers. He is still legally the head of the family, and the wife is unable, for example, to dispose of any property belonging to the family, except with the permission of the courts.

A much-resented burden for French mothers is that schools are compulsorily closed on Thursdays. The official reason for this is that an unbroken five-day week is considered too tiring for children. Whether this is true or not, a working mother finds herself faced with the outstanding problem of providing care for the children on Thursdays. It was found by a Government survey that in only 27 per cent of such families were the children placed under any form of organised supervision. In 47 per cent the children 'stayed at home', in 21 per cent recourse was had to 'children's groups', while in 5 per cent the children simply went out without supervision of any kind.

To encourage women to stay at home the French tax authorities operate what is known as 'single salary allowance'; this is forfeited if the wife earns more than one-third of her husband's salary. In fact the allowance is too small to have the desired effect and, whatever the law may have intended, the result has been not that mothers have remained at home, but that, needing to earn, they have worked illegally, without informing the authorities, so as not to lose the allowance. Women who work under such conditions are completely at the mercy of their employers.

On the other hand, it should be remembered that, although the English now seem to consider themselves daringly progressive in planning to change the law so that the breakdown of marriage shall become sufficient grounds for divorce,[6] this has always been the situation in France, generally supposed to be illiberal in such matters. French law is more civilised than British in this respect. It is sufficient grounds for divorce for a man to leave his family. Adultery does not have to be proved, there is no naming of co-respondents and neither party is required to ask the court's discretion in respect of his or her own adultery. Should either the husband or the wife refuse to agree to it, however, divorce in France can be a slower and more expensive affair than in Britain.

In the United States, the Equal Employment Opportunity Commission, most of whose work has centred round racial discrimination, has been increasing its role as arbiter of the equality of the sexes, as laid down in the Civil Rights Act. In 1965 the Commission issued what were described as 'new guideline interpretations on sex discrimination'.[7] These made it clear that any refusal to employ women because of 'assumptions of the comparative employment characteristics of women in general' would be strongly challenged by the Commission. It would not tolerate 'stereotyped characterisations of the sexes', especially that women are 'less capable of aggressive salesmanship' than men. This is important in a community where the business virtues are supreme. One result of the Commission's statement was that classified advertisements for sales staff increasingly began to carry the note 'An Equal Opportunity Employer'. As a further weapon the Commission warned that it would not honour State laws which served as barriers against rather than protection for women workers.

One makes these international comparisons partly in order to puncture British smugness, where this action seems called for, and partly to encourage the counting of blessings. In no country of the world is government so just and so wise, and the social situation so fortunate, that it is impossible for a woman to feel aggrieved about discrimination. To some extent, these injustices exist only in the eye of the beholder. One does not need to be a woman in order to feel, or indeed to be, persecuted or exploited, and the dedicated campaigner gleans ammunition for the cause in unlikely places. Yet an impartial observer, if such a person is possible within a field where emotions run so high, is bound, even in the enlightened permissive 1960s, to find many examples of outrageous prejudice and unfair discrimination with women as the victims. Careful reading of *The Times* and *The Guardian* alone will provide a daily ration of anti-feminist items culled from the world's news, although in most cases the people mentioned in the reports or responsible for writing them would probably deny holding anti-feminist views.

A *Times* obituary, for instance, was headed 'Miss Ann Redpath. A distinguished woman painter', and began, 'Miss Ann Redpath (Mrs Michie) had a deservedly high reputation as one of the most distinguished women painters of Britain in recent times.' 'In some ways,' the writer went on, 'her work might be compared to that of another distinguished woman painter, Ethel Walker, but it had an individuality which always caused it to stand out among the varied contributions to the mixed show'.[8] Few readers of *The Times* can have been in much doubt that someone called Miss Ann Redpath was a woman. Why then was it felt necessary to refer to her as a distinguished *woman* painter? Either she was distinguished as a painter or she was not. The implication is that women painters, as a category, are inferior to men, and that the best that can be said for Miss Redpath and Miss Walker is that they were outstanding members of the second eleven. 'The mixed show' suggests an event not unlike the mixed doubles at Wimbledon, with the men playing a more powerful game and the women included for mere variety. One almost expects the women's paintings there to have had distinctive frames. Yet such hostile reactions would have surprised the journalist responsible for Miss Redpath's obituary. As a member of the staff of *The Times* he was working within a long-established tradition, obeying the convention that it was somewhat remarkable that women should be painting at all.

The most innocent of arrangements can of course appear violently anti-feminist to anyone on the look-out for prejudice. When in 1965 a London publisher advertised *Mainly for Wives: a Practical Guide to Love-making*, by Robert Chartham, a feminist might have asked why a man should take it on himself to write a book where a woman's point of view and a woman's personal experience might be thought of some importance; why, in this of all matters, should women require man-made guidance? Or was 'Robert Chartham' a pseudonym covering a female author? Then, in 1966 a woman was charged at Middlesex Area Sessions with being drunk in charge of a car.[9] The deputy chairman felt that the circumstances demanded a mixed jury. 'I think it is undesirable,' he said, 'that a lady should be tried by an all-male jury. I feel in the public interest it is important that there should be ladies on a jury trying a lady.' The accused eventually faced ten men and two women, which demonstrates either that men always succeed in controlling everything, even in 1966, or alternatively that the male stranglehold on juries has been broken at last.

I have been collecting evidence of this kind for nearly ten years, much of it from newspapers and periodicals. The task seemed virtually thrust upon me when I worked as an industrial correspondent with the BBC, a job providing unlimited opportunities to study the conditions in which women work and to see a little way inside the minds of industrialists and politicians. That women were in practice still having a raw deal, that the possibilities of true human partnership were still largely unexplored, whatever the suffragettes may have achieved, was an inescapable conclusion. It appeared too that many men, whether employers or merely husbands, including some who could be expected to have the capacity to appreciate evidence daily before their eyes, still believed that women's wish to follow careers and to work outside their homes was no more than a temporary fashion. Given patience and goodwill and a steady increase in male earning power, the habit would disappear and women would gradually return to the domestic existence for which God had fashioned them. This book is written partly in an attempt to convince men nostalgic for the days of unquestioned male domination that women will increasingly and inevitably choose for themselves the kind of life they are going to lead, and that it is only common sense that they should be encouraged to do so. It seems not inappropriate that their case should be stated by a man. As John Stuart Mill wrote a hundred years ago in his very un-Victorian book *The Subjection of Women*, 'Women cannot be expected to devote themselves to the emancipation of women, until men in considerable numbers are prepared to join with them in the undertaking'.

ONE

The Roots of Anti-Feminism

Sir Winston Churchill is reported to have said that Lady Astor's entry into the House of Commons was tantamount to surprising him in his bath, the implication being that Lady Astor was somewhere she had no business to be.[1] Lady Astor had been elected on 28 November 1919 for the Sutton Division of Plymouth, at a by-election caused by her husband's accession to the peerage. 'Men whom I had known for years,' she recorded long afterwards, 'would not speak to me if they passed me in the corridors. They said I would not last six months. But I stuck it out.' Sir Winston's feelings were certainly not peculiar to himself.

Parliament is only one of many centres of male power where the intrusion of women has caused traditionalists to feel that the natural order of the universe has been overthrown and that nothing but decadence, decline and chaos lies ahead. Yet it has been in the great male club of Parliament and on the bench of bishops that educated men have been least reticent about publicly revealing their determination to keep women in their divinely ordained domestic purdah. *Hansard,* between 1880 and 1920, is an unequalled mine of anti-feminist remarks of a type still with us today. The traditionalists were never more outspoken than during the debate of 11 July 1910 on what had become an almost annual proposal to allow women a limited franchise. This particular debate is virtually a charter of the anti-feminist crusade in its pre-1914 form. It gave opportunities for rhetoric to a number of the most reactionary

Notes to this chapter are on page 168

members of the House, together with several of the more tolerant—and the better informed. Sir John Rolleston found it 'inconceivable' that a woman should ever be elected to Parliament and was certain that 'the women themselves'—the use of the definite article is interesting—wanted no such thing. Lord Hugh Cecil wisely and typically decided that women were not a sex at all, 'but a heterogeneous crowd of individuals of various miscellaneous opinions'. He was in favour of giving them the vote, and spoke of 'the dignified, the serene, and the emphatically womanly function of putting a mark on a piece of paper, and dropping it into a ballot box'. Yet he, too, was opposed to women becoming MPs, although he was unusually honest about his reasons: it would change the whole atmosphere of the House and spoil its traditions, of which he admitted he was proud. 'Everyone knows that a mixed assembly of the two sexes is always a different thing to an assembly confined to one sex. That is well known in school. It is well known at dinner parties.'

Arthur Balfour put forward a more ingenious argument. Women found it impossible to compromise: what they felt to be right had somehow to be put into practice without delay. This, Balfour conceded, was a noble aim and one which might well die of neglect in a world made up entirely of men. 'Women's moral mission,' as he saw it, 'is to keep burning the flame of the ideal in life and conduct, to keep burning those ideals of right for which we are all striving, in political as in other matters. It has been well said that, in politics, the ideal statesman is the man who knows what is right but does not force it unless it is expedient, and who knows what is expedient but does not force it unless it is right,' and such statesmenlike qualities were essentially male qualities. In Parliament, he believed, Members were compelled to breathe 'a continual atmosphere of compromise as little favourable to our ideals as is the ideally ventilated air of this chamber to our physical health. The intervention of woman in politics will tend either to make impossible the business of Government, or to extinguish in woman those ideals which are her most precious possession.'

Lord Haldane, Secretary of State for War, was in favour of women having the vote: the time would come 'when people will look back on the state of things in which we have drawn this political distinction between men and women with as much amazement as they look back upon the period when slavery was a recognised institution and held to be of the very foundation and of the essence of the well-being of the State.' Later generations, he was convinced, 'will feel that our doubts were the outcome of a great superstition, and will marvel that humanity had not emancipated itself earlier.' And the War Office, one remembers, was an exceedingly masculine citadel.

Hilaire Belloc assured the House that he yielded to nobody in his admiration for the intelligence of women. Only one category of men, in his view, believed that the intelligence of women was inferior to that of men. 'That category is only to be found amongst the very young unmarried men. As their experience of life increases, the judgment of men with regard to the intelligence of women passes from reverence to stupor and from stupor to terror'—a view which was also held by Dr Johnson, whom Boswell, in his *Journal of a Tour to the Hebrides*, reported as having said: 'Men know that women are an overmatch for them and therefore they choose the weakest or the most ignorant. If they did not think so, they could never be afraid of women knowing as much as themselves.' But Belloc was not in agreement with those who believed these terrifyingly intelligent beings should have the vote.

F. E. Smith, later Lord Birkenhead, sided with Belloc to the extent of admitting that it was not reasonable to base one's argument on 'some assumed inferiority of women'.[2] He was, however, perfectly prepared to say 'that the sum total of human happiness, knowledge and achievement would have been almost unaffected if Sappho had never sung, if Joan of Arc had never fought, if Siddons had never played and if George Eliot had never written.' In his firm opinion men, not women, had changed the course of history and made nations what they were. Women were ill-informed about the nation's business. 'During centuries, in schools, in shops, the mill, the street, in clubs, in ale-houses—in all those places—men are continually rubbing shoulders with their fellows and discussing public affairs, acquiring that extraordinary adaptability in the exercise of the vote which has long been the pride of this country in its democratic institutions. No such opportunities are open to women.'

It was an impressive and totally dishonest piece of legal pleading, good to listen to and rubbish to read. In his familiar manner, without pausing to wonder if 'such opportunities' or their equivalent might or should be made available to women—that the lack of them was what the debate was about—or to admit even the possibility that some men with the franchise might be stupid or insufficiently briefed to cast their vote intelligently,[3] Smith attacked hard on two points where he felt bound to win. If women were to be given the vote, a situation could arise in which they might 'impose their views on an actual majority of the men'. A particularly frightful and by no means impossible prospect was that they might vote against national service or against war. 'Women,' he reminded the House, 'are, actually or potentially, against fighting. The significance of this point of view for this country must always be prodigious.'[4]

On the whole, Smith was probably right in this view (although the bellicosity of some women once a war has broken out is frightening to experience). Beatrice Webb certainly supported the idea that women were by nature anti-war. She insisted that people would never understand the feminist movement until they realised that it was not mere feminism. She saw it as part of a general movement towards partnership among human beings, and linked it with the ideals implicit in the international labour movement and with the spreading revolt against colonialism. Maude Royden makes a similar point in her book *The Church and Women*, where she insists that any religion or society which bases itself on militarism and physical force must in its very nature be opposed to the freedom and authority of women. 'There is an instinct,' she says, 'which convinces us that those who bear life should not be life's destroyers.' Vera Brittain has put the same view equally forcibly: 'War violates a profound biological urge in women. The woman who shouts for war, whatever her temporary gain, has been perverted by propaganda from her natural instinct to create and to save.'[5] She notes that the military values which have come to dominate most twentieth-century states are inevitably prejudicial, if not hostile, to women's interests, because money spent on armaments cannot be used for improving health, education and welfare.

It is interesting to see the closeness of the link between the wish for a strong army and the opposition to votes for women in the case of Hilaire Belloc, whose contribution to the 1910 debate in the House of Commons has been mentioned. In his *Life of Hilaire Belloc* (1957), Robert Speaight reports Belloc as saying: 'I am opposed to women voting as men vote. I call it immoral, because I think the bringing of one's women, one's mothers and sisters and wives, into the political arena disturbs the relations between sexes.' In spite of, or because of, his mother's campaign for women's rights, Belloc was, decides Robert Speaight, 'a domestic diehard and thought that a woman's place was the home.'

He was also a remarkably self-confident military diehard, with a simple creed. 'It is common sense that any citizen of any country should wish that country to be strong, he should wish it to be self-respecting, powerful and happy. To this end I am for a strong Army and, by the way, a well-paid and a national Army. I believe it is absolutely necessary that we should keep our possessions with pride and security. The Empire is there, and it is our duty to retain it.' Until the 1920s, when the British Empire began its rapid decline, the Belloc-F. E. Smith attitude towards politics as an Army-inspired male club was normal. As expressed in the illuminating, if not illuminated, question put by J. A. Grant, Member for West Cumberland, in the Parliamentary debate of May 1913 on franchise reform: 'In controlling a vast Empire like our own, an Empire built by the mental and physical capacity of men, and maintained, as it always must be maintained, by the physical and mental capacities of masterly natures—I ask myself: Is there a place for women?'

Since war and the preparation for war is at the centre of the philosophy of the nation-state, and since Britain's expansion overseas was based on the unfeminine qualities of violence and aggression, the Victorians and Edwardians had some incentive to keep women from public affairs, where they were likely to threaten the priorities and values held by so many men. War is the culmination of childish delinquency, the most extreme form of male violence, and women who oppose it, within Parliament or elsewhere, arouse in the adult child a store of half-suppressed memories of reproofs by mother or schoolmistress. This resentment can even, occasionally, find blatantly melodramatic outlet, as explained by a twelve-year-old boy brought before a juvenile court in Somerset for attacking a young woman walking down a dark lane: 'I did scare the lady. I did it because when we were younger we got lots of hits and slaps from women and girls. I did it to scare her.'[6]

So women, it was felt, must continue to find their satisfactions in what F. E. Smith nauseatingly, but one hopes sincerely, described as 'the true functions of womanhood faithfully discharged', and as the guardians of 'the tenderest and most sacred influences which animate mankind'. Whether women wished to confine themselves to small domestic paddocks was beside the point. It was their duty to do so and it was for their own good. Smith, like so many of his contemporaries, was terrified at the prospect of the New Woman, but as usual the artists understood what was happening long before the politicians did. Henry James's novel *The Bostonians* appeared in 1886. In his introduction to the 1952 edition, Lionel Trilling paints a convincing picture of James terrified by the approach of 'a feminine, a nervous, hysterical, chattering, canting age, an age of which the ultimate horror was to be the spectacle of the sacred mothers refusing their commission'. His New Women, Fleda Vetch, Willy Theale, Isobel Archer and so on, were incarnations of the horror. In this matter at least, F. E. Smith and Henry James would have found little to divide them.

This paternalism—it was precisely that—produced something very close to a split mind on the part of many educated men during the later nineteenth and early twentieth centuries. On the one hand we have the ludicrous protective attitude towards women of their own social level—working-class women were regarded as a different breed altogether—and on the other a willingness to resort to the most brutal treatment if these same frail, publicly idolised creatures should, as erring children, happen to show any sign of demanding equal rights with men. One of the choicest examples from the utterances of the protect-our-women school comes from a paper read by Mr Justice Beaman to a ladies' circle in 1908, and later printed: 'As the fairest, daintiest natural thing will not brook rough handling or too close and continued examination, the iridescence of the butterfly's wing, the velvet of the rose petal, so the rare and exquisite essence of womanliness will not bear the heat, the mud, the profanation of the public arena.'

Once the fragile butterfly had invaded the public arena, however, she found no holds barred in the male determination to push her back into her cage, as Lady Constance Lytton found to her cost. Lady Constance was forcibly fed in prison, as part of her punishment for engaging in suffragette activities, although her exalted social station was not realised at the time she was tortured. The scene has been precisely described by Sylvia Pankhurst in her book *The Suffragette*:

'The doctor then produced a wooden and a steel gag and told her that he would not use the latter, which would hurt, unless she resisted him; but as she would not unlock her teeth he threw the milder wooden instrument aside and prised her mouth open with the steel one. Then the stomach tube was forced down and the whole hateful feeding business was gone through. "It was a living nightmare of pain, horror and revolting degradation", she said. "The sense is of being strangled, suffocated by the thrust down of the large rubber tube, which arouses great irritation in the throat and nausea in the stomach.

The anguish and effort of retching whilst the tube is forcibly pressed back into the stomach and the natural writhing of the body restrained defy description".' This punishment still goes on. Miss Pat Arrowsmith, a pacifist and an advocate of nuclear disarmament, was forcibly fed in Holloway Prison in 1962.

It was, as Mary Stott has recently written, 'a glimpse of the beastliness of Men when their dominance is threatened.'[7] Protests against male domination had been made for getting on for a century before the suffragettes brought matters to a head. In 1825, for instance, William Thompson published a book in which he advanced powerful arguments against the exclusion of women from all say in politics. The title was as forthright as anything produced by the suffragettes: *An appeal of one half of the human race, Women, against the pretensions of the other half, Men, to retain them in political, and thence in Civil and domestic slavery*. Below the title, Thompson summarised the book's contents in a pungent couplet:

> 'Tis all duty on the female side
> On men's, mere sensual lust and surly pride.

The book was forcefully written. Its simple theme was that married women were slaves. 'Home is the eternal prison-house of the wife. The husband paints it as the abode of calm bliss, but takes care to find out of doors, for his own use, a species of bliss not quite so calm . . . The house is his with everything in it, and of all fixtures the most abjectly his is his breeding machine, the wife.' Only by political equality could women escape from the tyranny of men which reduced them to 'the condition of Negroes in the West Indies'. Acting as their self-appointed spokesman, Thompson insisted that women 'ask every facility of access to every art, occupation, profession, from the highest to the lowest. They ask the removal of all restraints and exclusions not applicable to men of similar capacities.'

This was of course a sweeping exaggeration. 'Women' is a large concept and Thompson had no means of knowing what 'women' asked. The evidence suggests that a large proportion of English women during the past two centuries and more have always been willing to accept the inferior role so plainly emphasised in the Old Testament and by St Paul, and neatly described and justified by Milton in *Samson Agonistes*:

> Therefore God's universal law
> Gave to the man despotic power
> Over his female in due awe
> Nor from that right to part an hour
> Smile she or lour.

The equally respectable Christian precept that 'in Christ is neither male nor female' never seems to have earned much attention. It has certainly never persuaded the Anglican Church Assembly to accept women for the priesthood, although some of the Nonconformist churches have been more liberal. The Church Assembly is a strong candidate for the title of the most anti-feminist body in Britain. Its post-war debates on the admission of women to the Ministry have often had an incredibly nineteenth-century flavour, and have been strangely lacking in gratitude when one recalls that Church of England congregations are overwhelmingly female.

Thirty years earlier than Milton, Sir Thomas Browne in a celebrated passage in *Religio Medici* had expressed the same attitude more appealingly but equally forcefully. 'The whole World is made for Man,' he declared, 'but the twelfth part for Woman. Man is the whole World and the Breath of GOD; Woman the Rib and crooked Piece of Man . . . I speak not in prejudice, nor am averse from that sweet Sex, but naturally amorous of all that is beautiful.' *Playboy* is much in the Sir Thomas Browne tradition. Even educated women accepted this permanent, God-given relegation to an inferior status. In 1838 Caroline Norton, a granddaughter of Richard Brinsley Sheridan, and a considerable authoress herself, wrote 'I for one (I and millions more) believe in the natural superiority of man as I believe in the existence of God.'

Apart from the sheer problem of collecting an adequate

body of information, the difficulty and absurdity lurking in so many arguments either way about women's thoughts or wishes is the assumption that all men resemble one another and that all women are necessarily different from all men. The point of view one adopts must to a large extent depend on the people one knows. There are superior men and inferior men, just as there are intelligent and capable women and stupid feckless women, but the politician and the demagogue find it tactically rewarding to treat all members of a group as identical beings and to make the group as monolithic as possible.

A not uncommon type is the woman who prefers to identify herself with men, on the grounds that female company is moronic and boring. Baroness Asquith (Lady Violet Bonham-Carter) appears to fall into this category. In her book *Winston Churchill as I knew him* she reveals herself as a passionate Churchill-worshipper. Churchill was a man whose 'inner circle of friends contained no women'; it is clear that she regarded herself as qualifying for friendship by being an untypical woman. Her attitude towards her own sex is suggested by an entry in her diary for June 1915, when she was setting up an Admiralty Information Bureau in Alexandria. 'It is such a comfort,' she wrote, 'to be working with hard-headed, busy, professional men, instead of soft-hearted, idle fuddled women.' The antithesis is absurd and unjust. Even in 1915 and among the English middle-class, only a small minority of men can have been hard-headed, busy and professional, and only a small minority of women soft-hearted, idle and fuddled.

Lady Asquith was, of course, Asquith's daughter and liable to judge people by strict standards, with a particular scorn for the mentally flabby. Dislike of feminine tittle-tattle must always have been a major cause of anti-feminism among men unfortunate enough not to have known more intelligent women. But masculine tittle-tattle is just as common and infuriating, although not so frequently labelled for what it is. One wonders what Lady Asquith's attitude would have been towards the female floggers and mutilators envisaged by Lady

Bathurst in 1913 as being the proper people to deal with women claiming political rights. Her recipe does not reveal a very agreeable subconscious, but at least it can hardly be termed soft-hearted. 'When a suffragette has been convicted, first have her well birched, by women, then shave off her hair, and finally deport her to New Zealand or Australia.' No man could have said it better. Neither sex, of course, has a monopoly of any of the human qualities, although it is probable that certain combinations of qualities, not necessarily desirable, are found more frequently among men than among women, and vice-versa. The idea fascinated many writers and thinkers in Victorian times and is commonplace today. Tennyson, influenced by some of the ideas of Owenite socialism, believed that as society progressed the crude distinction between men and women would begin to disappear.

> Yet in the long years liker they must grow,
> The man be more of woman, she of man.[8]

The old-style psychologists were divided on the matter. Havelock Ellis urged the similarity of the sexes, in the style of the late eighteenth and early nineteenth century rationalists, and the falseness of the distinction between 'masculine' and 'feminine'. Freud, on the other hand, preached the Victorian doctrine of the difference of the two sexes and the importance of male domination.

Coleridge said that the great mind is androgynous, that male and female characteristics have become fused within it. Pondering on this Virginia Woolf found herself enquiring if perhaps 'a mind that is fully masculine cannot create, any more than a mind that is purely feminine'.[9] Shakespeare's mind, she felt, may be taken as 'the type of androgynous, of the man-womanly mind'. Pursuing the thought, she says, 'If it be true that it is one of the tokens of the fully developed mind that it does not think specially or separately of sex, how much harder it is to attain that condition now [1929] than ever before . . . No age can ever have been as stridently sex-conscious as our own; those innumerable books by men about women in the

British Museum are a proof of it. The Suffrage campaign was no doubt to blame. It must have roused in men an extraordinary desire for self-assertion; it must have made them lay an emphasis upon their own sex and its characteristics which they would not have troubled to think about had they not been challenged. And when one is challenged, even by a few women in black bonnets, one retaliates, if one has never been challenged before, rather excessively.'[10]

J. B. Priestley has campaigned against man-woman labels for many years, insisting that such crude distinctions impoverish and distort politics, the arts and social life, and prevent people from growing properly as individuals. 'I am convinced that good talk cannot flourish where there is a wide gulf between the sexes, where the men are altogether too masculine, too hearty and bluff and booming, where the women are too feminine, at once both too arch and too anxious. Where men are leavened by a feminine element, where women are not without some tempering by the masculine spirit, there is a chance of good talk.'[11]

In America, Mr Priestley found a society 'entirely dominated by the masculine spirit'. Women were 'haunted by a feeling of inferiority, resented but never properly examined and challenged. They lived in a world so contemptuous and destructive of real feminine values that they had to be heavily bribed to remain in it.' American women may often be 'so aggressive, demanding, dictatorial, that many men are only happy when they can get away from them,' but this is misleading. America, he writes, is only superficially a matriarchy. 'Life in America is dominated by the masculine and not the feminine principle . . . If women become aggressive, demanding, dictatorial, it is because they find themselves struggling to find satisfaction in a world that is not theirs. If they use sex as a weapon, it is because they so badly need a weapon. They are like the inhabitants of an occupied country. They are compelled to accept values and standards that are alien to their deepest nature.'[12] Woman projects on to individual men 'her unconscious resentment of the triumphant masculine principle' and men, in their turn, 'are baffled and miserable, telling one another that women have always been like this, not knowing what they want, the crazy creatures. But woman does know what she wants, and has always been the saner partner. It is the society these men have created, are still creating, that does not know what it wants and is lunatic. It is the society of the hydrogen bomb.'

Some of us might feel that the most agreeable people we meet seem to possess a strong streak of the opposite sex and that, conversely, the most difficult or demanding people are either 100 per cent male or 100 per cent female.[13] This idea is anathema to those who see human destiny as inevitably expressed in terms of wars and violence. For them the non-aggressive, unbrutalised male, despising violence, is an undesirable fellow citizen, to be impatiently brushed aside. The fact that the methods of the extreme types of male and female may be obsolescent is ignored. The Man Who Gets Things Done continues to be presented as the ideal human prototype, crass and brutal as he may prove on close examination. Churchill and Lloyd George, both great popular heroes in their time, had an urgent fanatical desire to get things done, confident that God had appointed them to carry out the tasks that faced them. Churchill, in particular, had a ruthless, inhuman side, an aspect which Graham Sutherland caught so brilliantly in his much-reviled painting. His public career was all-important to him and nothing could be allowed to stand between him and his destiny. He had that highly dangerous quality, the artistic temperament turned to the conduct of public affairs, and his egocentricity, bloody-mindedness and waywardness were its natural consequence.

Very few women can have seen their own political career in such terms and it is small wonder that Churchill, who was essentially a war leader—that essentially masculine type of politician—should have viewed the entry of women into Parliament with such grim forebodings. Women stand for the wrong things, even for dangerously wrong things. They are liable to think people more important than the Nation; capable of intense loyalty to individuals, even unworthy individuals, they can rarely muster much loyalty to an institution, which of course increases male reluctance to offer them key posts.

To the two main reasons for keeping women out of public life during most of the nineteenth century and more than half of the twentieth—men's fear of the introduction of a different scale of values into the conduct of the nation's business both at home and abroad, and their fear, almost as keen, for the end of their own domestic domination and domestic comforts—it is necessary to add one or two more sources of anti-feminism which have become important since the end of the first world war and the granting of the vote to women.

Before 1914, there was no question of women filling important positions in industry or commerce, fields where male values predominated as completely as in foreign policy. Since then, however, there has been a very similar process of trying to exclude women from any but comparatively minor executive jobs on the grounds that they would not be sufficiently hard, ruthless, unscrupulous and single-minded to fight and beat down competitors or to control potentially rebellious labour. Business is a form of war and, as such, an unsuitable field of employment for women. There is something in this theory, although perhaps not as much as its protagonists imagine. Some businesses are run successfully on less bellicose lines; and a combination of the differing approaches of both sexes can give a business stability and strength. In any case there are, after all, many different types of women, and training and acclimatisation can accomplish much.

More men than women, however, feel a strong compulsion to reach controlling positions in whatever their field of work may be, partly from an enjoyment of power itself and its prestige, and partly as a means of protecting themselves during their fifties and sixties, assuming the pressure of business allows them to live so long. This, in itself, has produced a new form of male resentment, a rivalry, where women are concerned.

As a result of fairly reliable, if not foolproof, contraceptives the emancipation of women is now a reality. In England or America, at least, women are not often forced to have children they do not want; their breeding habits are, or can be, under their personal control. We might therefore be entering the dream age of sexual equality and genuine companionship that generations of feminists struggled to achieve. Yet this very emancipation has produced entirely new problems, as serious as those displaced. Although women now have freedom to educate themselves, to train for a chosen occupation and to compete in the labour market, they are also free, in a way most men are not, to pull out of a career and settle for a home and family once their job begins to bore them or when they appear to have reached the limit of their capabilities.

As a Swedish writer has put it, 'Women have it too easy. In a highly competitive society, where men are driven to ulcers and heart attacks by fear of professional failure, it is indeed a great privilege to be able to set out on a career knowing, as women do, that if they do not succeed they lose face neither as human beings nor as women. People may not even know if a woman fails: she may get married and pretend she "sacrificed her career" in order to make a good home. Woman's body has always been her foremost means of subsistence. It still is. Even married women with a career usually have a higher standard of living than their own income would give them. They are usually married to men who make more money than they do themselves. To a great extent this is due to earlier injustices, but it is also due to the fact that women do not take their career as seriously as men do. They do not see work and professional achievement as a necessary part of human existence, but rather as something they should have the right to devote themselves to *if they feel like it*.'[14]

This is a freedom which escapes men, who are compelled to continue working until they finally retire. In addition to this an even greater injustice hangs over their heads. Since contraception is increasingly decided and controlled by women, men can be much more easily tricked or compelled into marriage and, on the other hand, they can no longer resort to their traditional method of exercising domination over women, forcing them to have children and consequently to remain at home.

Yet to suggest that the more men and women are free to choose the sort of life they want to lead, the less different they are is obviously absurd. When false inequalities vanish, the genuine differences appear. Among today's famous married couples, nearly always both husband and wife have jobs. This certainly dissolves the erstwhile difference between the man of action and the woman who knows only her own four walls, but it does nothing to change the fundamental relationship between masculinity and femininity, between men and women. The French writer Claude Roy has discussed this problem with a number of well-known actresses. His findings are interesting.[15] Marguerite Duras, for instance, was convinced that 'We need to be dependent on a man.' Simone Signoret echoed this; 'I should find it very difficult to do without the domination of a man, without obedience to a man;' and Jeanne Moreau had a similar approach: 'I don't think I could love a man without admiring him first.' Claude Roy comments: 'Three very intelligent women, all with work that makes them happy and independent, all re-invent the model of lord and master.' Research among equally successful and apparently independent Englishwomen would almost certainly produce similar results.

The desire for a lord and master is deeply ingrained, though it would not be easy to find the modern equivalent of Vera Brittain's Victorian father, who emphasised his natural superiority when taking his wife and children away for their summer holiday by travelling first class himself but sending them third.[16] Nor would today's feelings be represented by those of the foreman cleaner in Finsbury, aged forty-eight, who was sent to prison in January 1960 for injuring his wife by throwing a plate at her, having said to a detective that a man had a right to chastise his wife. 'That utterly contemptible theory,' said the magistrate, 'comes from the Middle Ages and the jungles of pre-civilisation.' So, presumably, does that of the lorry driver of Metz, in France, who in 1963 literally chained his wife to the sink every morning and released her on his return from work in the evening, adding a lorry-engine piston to each of her ankles for added security.

There is and will be no end to the theories advanced to account for hostility and suspicion between the sexes. A number of the more prevalent will be discussed in the following chapters. Psychology has endless dark suggestions. Meanwhile we may usefully note that, by turning the well-worn Freudian theory of women's penis-envy on its head, Geoffrey Gorer and others have suggested that the apparently never-ending conflict between men and women has its origins in the male's need to bolster his morale by means of practical and observable achievements of some kind in order to compensate for his inability to bear children. This causes him to try to discover activities which are possible only to men, and to ensure that the female is a mother and nothing else. Once women have the power to refuse motherhood, the main source of male domination has gone.

Perhaps men have not noticed, however, that when tied down as mothers, many women have still contrived to assert their authority and sow the seeds of future resentment in a peculiarly lasting fashion. In America especially, women frequently have their male children circumcised as a matter of course. It is the one way in which a superficially matriarchal society can permanently influence the physical characteristics of the males. The motive is quite different from that behind the religious, male-directed, obligation of Jewish and Moslem communities. The mother-inspired circumcision cult among white Americans is not paralleled in Britain, although it has occurred, as a fashion rather than as a cult, among upper and upper-middle class Englishwomen for several generations now. These are also the families which send their sons to boarding schools; and there may well be a connection between the two habits.

But theories such as Geoffrey Gorer's are mere froth on the surface. Within western civilisation men are trying to re-adjust themselves to a society in which their own role is completely different from the one which was normal and traditional up till at least the beginning of the present century. They find themselves faced with two dilemmas. The first is how to reconcile today's sedentary, mechanised existence with the ancient image of the male as one whose destiny is to meet physical challenges, and the second is how to reconcile the democratic theories of the present, which emphasise equal rights for women, with the patriarchal image of man as provider and protector.

This struggle to discover a satisfying identity, or indeed any identity at all, makes many men feel sexually insecure. Until recently this insecurity was overcome in one of two ways, according to the prevailing view of the female sex drive. For most of the historical period, woman has been assumed to be a sexually voracious creature who needed to be kept under strict control. The Victorians tried a new approach. They ignored or denied the idea of enormous female sexuality, and established a new convention, that woman's sex drive was much weaker than man's, if it existed at all, and that respectable women found no enjoyment at all in sexual intercourse.

Modern man is confronted with an entirely different situation, in which women are acknowledged to have strong sexual needs which society approves rather than deprecates. This may create difficulties for him, arising mainly from a doubt as to whether he is capable of giving a democratically-demanding woman the satisfaction she expects. As Myron Brenton has said in his book *The American Male* (1967), 'The girl who is candid about her own sex desires appears sexually menacing, rather than sexually exciting.' The matter is made worse by the publication of books and articles of the Kinsey Report type, which provides a stupefying quantity of statistics about both male and female sexuality and, in a competitive society, force a man to compare his performance with that of other men. The struggle to keep up may seem intolerable and pointless, with the result that men find relief either in homosexuality—there are estimated to be at least two million homosexuals in the United States today—or with prostitutes. Brenton's researches lead him to conclude that 'a great many men, and quite likely the majority of men, are able to function at peak level sexually only with women who are submissive, or skilfully pretend to accept the domination of the male . . . Increasingly, the men who require the services of prostitutes say they have wives who are too responsive and demanding.'

Some men resent women's new-found equality so strongly that they will welcome any opportunity to put the clock back, and to return to a more primitive and acceptable form of life. *Playboy* magazine has based its tremendous success on this widely-found nostalgia for the period when men knew where they were. The *Playboy* prescription for happiness, repeated, stressed and illustrated in every issue, is the traditional one of woman as man's plaything, to be picked up and discarded at will and without sentiment. The classic method of escape from over-demanding, over-controlling women is, of course, war and the military life. In Britain, as in Western Europe as a whole, the man-is-a-warrior stereotype is not very popular nowadays; but it is widely accepted in America and Australia, so that anyone campaigning for peace there is made to appear effeminate and vaguely subversive. Fear and dislike of violence is taken to represent a specifically feminine influence and to mark the beginning of a dangerous weakening in the national character.

Yet many men are strongly opposed to violence and, on certain occasions, many women exhibit characteristics which are not in the stereotype at all. 'Anyone who has seen the twisted faces of some of the women who attend prizefights and wrestling matches, faces contorted with the lust for blood: anyone who has witnessed the hate-filled glitter in the eyes of women on both sides of the fence at a racial clash: anyone who has borne the brunt of corrupting bitterness that flows from some of the female activists in the camps of political extremism: and anyone who has observed the frenzy of women at a rummage sale—anyone who, for that matter, has read a history of the feminist movement—might well have understandable doubts about the gentler sex necessarily being so gentle, the loving sex necessarily being so loving.'[17] The elimination of war and the development of a society based on humane and co-operative values cannot be achieved so long as such values are written off as feminine. They are asexual, and to pretend otherwise is irresponsible and escapist.

Two notable books about American militarism and the Vietnam war appeared in 1967. One was written by a former sergeant in the American Special Services and the other by an American woman journalist and novelist. They show the same attitude to the war and the political situation and they stand up for civilised values in precisely the same way. The writers' sex is irrelevant and many parts of both books could have been written by either person. The reader may like to guess from any evidence he pleases whether the author of the following passages was Mary McCarthy or Donald Duncan.

> The country needs to understand that the war is wrong, and the sole job of the opposition should be to enforce that understanding and to turn it, wherever possible, into the language of action. It is clear that US senators and former ambassadors are not going to sit in at the Pentagon or hurl themselves at troop trains; nobody expects that of them, and nobody seriously expects elected or appointed officials to practise tax refusal. But one could expect practical support for the young people who are resisting the draft from a few courageous officeholders and from private figures with a genuine sense of public responsibility. The question is simple: Do I disapprove more of the sign that picket is carrying—and the beard he is wearing—or of the Vietnamese war? To judge by introspection, the answer is not pretty. For the middle-class, middle-aged 'protector', the war in Vietnam is easier to take than a sign that says 'Johnson murderer'.[18]

> The Congress and generations of tradition fought it out with the military after World War II and lost. The military not only forced the idea of a large standing military on a

people traditionally opposed to such an idea, but made them believe in its necessity. Universal Military Training was voted in ostensibly to maintain freedom and the American tradition, when in fact it was designed by the military to perpetuate itself.

The saturation of the civilian community by men accustomed to thinking in military terms has been so pervasive that we have lost the essentials necessary for absolute civilian control. Within the United States today, for all practical purposes, there is no separation of the communities and no difference in thinking. We have, in fact, military thinking in civilian clothing.

The process of changing a man into a soldier is brutalising, even if he never kills another, and, sadly, the individual seldom recognises his own brutalisation, his changing sense of values. The process of changing a nation into a military society is equally brutalising, and, just as sadly, few of its people recognise the transformation.[19]

Critics of the capitalist system have frequently said, as they have of the public-school system, that its main defect lies in what it does to people. The values of big business are not so very different from those of the army or the public school: the stiff upper lip, the subordination of personal feelings and personal relationships, the defeat of competitors by any method which society can be persuaded to accept, the determination to occupy enemy territory, the belief that the success of the enterprise is of more value than the happiness of individual employees, the propaganda screen to cover up operations which are better not observed too closely or too clearly, the coining of ever vaguer and nobler-sounding euphemisms to veneer uncivilised activities. Within a society whose values are those acceptable to business—and the United States is such a society—acquisitiveness is the supreme virtue and a man is judged, and judges himself, by his power to acquire.

One of the British productivity teams sent to pick up hints in the United States after World War II remarked on the key economic role played by wives. 'In this competition for a higher standard of life,' says the Report, 'it is undoubtedly the American woman who is the pacemaker. In the striving for higher wages, based on higher productivity, the American worker has unquestionably well "prepared himself unto the battle", and the trumpet sounded by his wife, and to which his unflagging efforts are often the valiant response, does not give an uncertain sound. Viewed from the standpoint of high national industrial productivity, the influence, in this way, of the American woman, must be regarded as distinctly valuable.'[20]

Valuable to the economy, possibly, but not necessarily to the encouragement of good relations between the sexes. So long as he can perform it to his own satisfaction—which includes his wife's satisfaction—a man's breadwinning role helps to confirm his manliness. If the driving process becomes too obvious, too insistent or too unreasonable, however, he may come to resent the woman for whose benefit he is killing himself. In recent years it has been increasingly common for American companies to send a copy of a salesman's figures home to his wife, pointing out that they are not what they might be and suggesting that a little domestic pressure might improve matters. The man is then in almost the same position as the boy whose parents confront him with an unsatisfactory school report. He has to account for himself—and the explanation is not between equals.

In America in particular many comfortably-off women appear and genuinely believe themselves to be wholly concerned with cultural values and with the general good of humanity. But their husbands are placed in an unenviable position, since on the one hand they are likely to be attacked for their obsession with money, their neglect of their family and their lack of interest in what their wives call culture, and on the other they are remorselessly driven on to earn the money to make wife-centred culture possible. In these cases, for all the female protestations, the wife and the husband have precisely the same basic values. The one difference between them is that the wife finds business values materialistic and offensive and sub-contracts them to her husband. This allows her the comfort of feeling better about herself, at the price of disliking or looking down on her husband.

It is not surprising that in recent years the Family Service Agency of Marin County in California has had to deal with a number of men who admit that they are envious of women's good fortune in not having to exhaust and degrade themselves in a highly competitive labour market, and say that they would like to reverse roles with their wives, so that they stayed at home and did the housework and their wives went out to earn the family living. Resentment against women could hardly go further.

The American Negroes have had for generations what the white clients of the Family Service Agency appear to be clamouring for now. Slavery inevitably made Negro society in America a matriarchy. Marriages meant little and husbands were often sold separately from their wives, so that the only meaningful link was between mother and child. This matriarchy continued after the end of slavery. The Negro woman found work fairly easily, either in a factory or in domestic service, but the Negro man was often unemployed. The wage-earning mother giving pin-money to her feckless husband is a central figure of the Negro myth in the United States, but the picture is solidly based on observable fact. Even today, Negro women tend to be better educated and to have better jobs than the men. This has had important political consequences, which have not always been recognised for what they are. As Andrew Sinclair has pointed out, 'the relative success of the Black Muslims among the poorer segments of Negro society can be explained as much in terms of the Negro man's revolt against the dominant Negro woman as by his revolt against the white man.'[21]

Not all observers have seen this aspect of the Black Muslim movement in the same way. Dr E. V. Essien-Udom, a Nigerian who has lived and taught for a number of years in the United States, and is now Professor of Political Science at Ibadan, believes that the Muslim movement, the Nation, is bringing great advantages to women. 'One of the principal motives which lead Negro women to join the Nation is their desire to escape from their position as women in Negro subculture. The attraction of the Nation of Islam to women becomes clear if we bear in mind that both men and women in the Nation extend a great deal of deference towards each other—something they are unaccustomed to in Negro society . . . The Muslim male's attitude towards, and treatment of, Negro women contrasts sharply with the disrespect and indifference with which lower-class Negroes treat them. Muhammad's semi-religious demand that his followers must respect the black woman has an appeal for black women seeking to escape from their lowly and humiliating position in Negro society and from the predatory sex ethos of the lower-class community. A refuge from these abuses is found in the Nation of Islam. It is a journey from shame to dignity.'[22]

TWO

The Education of Women

In 1966 Mr Philip Barford, lecturer in music in the extra-mural department of Liverpool University, wrote to *The Times*[1] about his experiences in adult education. He began: 'I am rapidly becoming convinced that love of beauty, thirst for experience, concern for intellectual adventure, the essential curiosity, the will to know and faith in the human spirit are predominantly feminine characteristics in modern British society.' Assuming that the situation described by Mr Barford is not peculiar to Lancashire, this is an allegation that culture in Britain is passing increasingly into feminine hands, that fewer girls than boys are mentally crippled by their formal education and that the education of girls pays a good deal more attention to the cultivation of civilised values.

Yet the majority view of people professionally concerned with education, especially as theorists, appears to run in precisely the opposite direction. The most commonly heard criticism is that the efforts of the nineteenth and twentieth century feminists to give girls equal education opportunities with boys have produced an educational system in which the girls become warped and frustrated precisely because they are educated as if they were boys. Sir John Newsom, after many years of educational administration, has come to hold this opinion very strongly. 'We try,' he says, 'to educate girls into being imitation men, and as a result we are wasting and frustrating their qualities of womanhood at great expense to the community. I believe that, in addition to their needs as individuals,

Notes to this chapter are on page 171

our girls should be educated in terms of their main social function—which is to make for themselves, their children and their husbands a secure and suitable home, and to be mothers.'[2]

In the same article Sir John explained what kind of education he had in mind, making it clear that it was to be an education for the generality of women, not merely for future cabinet ministers or Fellows of the Royal Society, and that it was in addition to those aspects of education designed to lead to a career. It should be planned, he believed, in terms of creating an intelligent and satisfying home environment. 'The job of being an intelligent wife and mother requires the highest possible sensitivity of a variety of kinds. It means being a bit of a psychologist, knowing the way the world works, how the local community functions, what the powers of the local authorities are, what social services are available for you and your family, and so on. It means—and this is increasingly important—knowing how to make an intelligent use of leisure. That means being able to read, to use books intelligently, perhaps to play and teach musical instruments, to be discriminating about what you listen to or view on television.'

This kind of education, Sir John emphasised, would cost the country more, not less, than it was paying at the moment, but it would provide better value for money, in the sense that it would enrich family life and remove much of the boredom and frustration that so many married women feel. One supposes that the women attending the extra-mural classes run by Mr Barford and others are attempting to broaden their minds in approximately the way advocated by Sir John Newsom, but in, of course, very small numbers. Two immediate comments suggest themselves, before we examine the female rage let loose on Sir John as a result of his article. The first is that boys appear to need an education of this kind every bit as much as girls. If their schooling is not to result in 'the highest possible sensitivity of a variety of kinds', there is surely something seriously wrong with it. The second thought is that it implies that, to be effective, the education of girls must cost more than the education of boys, and one shudders to think of the resentment that would cause and the political battle that would be needed to push it through. It may be, of course, that Sir John believes that all our present-day education is shoddy and ineffective, because we try to get it on the cheap, but that is another matter. It is curious, even so, to see the remarkable similarity of intention between what Sir John Newsom proposed in 1964 and the warrior's rest described by the Archbishop of York in 1863: 'When men, weary with the world's battle, return to the cool shade of their own homes, they need the calmness, the refinement, the high cultivation, the unselfishness, the gentle piety, which woman, as she was meant to be, knows how to afford him.'

The *Observer* invited five educated women who had been markedly successful in their careers, to comment on Sir John's article.[3] They all, in different degrees, seem to have found it patronising and reactionary.

Mrs Mary Stocks, now Baroness Stocks, thought Sir John was no doubt right in assuming that the life of a woman today is likely to involve 'an uncomfortable amalgam' of home-making and wage or salary-earning. 'Such a life,' she insisted, 'involves no pursuit of any craft up to high professional standard, no study in depth of any subject. It is a life inimical to mental concentration. And for such a life Sir John advocates an education on what can only be called finishing-school principles at *Reader's Digest* level. It is not *for* such a vocation that girls should be educated, but against it—in order to survive.' It is not, perhaps, irrelevant to mention in this context that Lady Stocks is on record as having said, in a broadcast made in September 1964: 'Most women dislike full-time domesticity.'

Margaret Miles, the headmistress of Mayfield Comprehensive School in London, felt that the argument should be broadened to include a greater variety of girls. Sir John's work-marriage-work pattern seemed slightly defeatist. She agreed it was perfectly true that a woman could not take up her career again 'as though it had not been interrupted', because one of the results of her being a woman was that it *had* been interrupted. 'But there she is at forty, her young in flight from the nest and with many years of active life before her. It could be just as bad for her not to have a trained skill to recover at this stage in her life, as it might have been for her not to have got married and had children at the earlier stage. And this is true not only of the 5 per cent of career women mentioned by Sir John.'

Marghanita Laski was in substantial agreement with Mary Stocks and came close to accusing Sir John of being an agent of the advertisers and manufacturers. 'In the last century,' she said, 'it was truly said that if you taught the ploughboy his letters he'd leave the plough; and though Sir John would be the last to wish it, he is on the side of those who believe that if you hold other than purely "feminine" ideals before women, they will be deflected from wasteful consumption. "Men want girls to be feminine like it says in *Vogue*," said a Girton girl recently on TV, and the potent female image of today is imposed by *Vogue* and its like to the point where correction, not enhancement, by the school is needed.'

Dr Kathleen Ollerenshaw, who has been chairman of Manchester's Education Committee, and is the author of a recent survey of girls' education, *The Girls' Schools*, thought that one of the best hopes for women was the developing trend among men for continued education and training. She believes in giving adults the opportunity to educate themselves. 'When we throw overboard our too slavish adherence in education to age-ranges; when study leaves, refresher and promotion courses are accepted and shared by women as normal, whether at twenty-five or thirty-five or forty-five; then at last will women find the intellectual nourishment that they may reject at sixteen but often crave for later. Then they will have a real chance, after bringing up children, of returning to work at levels that match their abilities.'[4]

The most thorough-going attack came from Katharine Whitehorn, a well-known and successful journalist and married with two young children. She found Sir John's proposals essentially anti-feminist. ' "Separate but equal" in this context,' she said, 'means exactly what it does in Alabama.' She opposed his plans if on no other ground than that she found it unrealistic to think the Government *would* pay as much money for girls if their education were considered as a separate issue. In her opinion the bulk of the intellectual exercises boys went through at school were no more vocationally suited to their job as males than to that of girls as females. Plato was no more the preserve of man because Plato was a man than he was the preserve of Greeks because Plato was a Greek.

In any case, she reminded her readers, education is supposed to be a corrective as well as an encouragement to natural enthusiasms. The fact that a lot of fifteen-year-old boys are interested only in football, guns and girls—in that order—is not taken as a reason for teaching them about nothing else. Sir John's list of domestic arts seemed to be hardly calculated to whet the intellectual curiosity—in fact it was more reminiscent of needlework and tinkling at the pianoforte, which had always been permitted to polite young ladies. If such hobbies at home had been enough to satisfy women they wouldn't have gone to such trouble to break out: they wanted something rather more demanding. And she felt that Sir John had not sufficiently considered what happens to women *after* they have raised their families.

Katharine Whitehorn put her cards on the table and declared that she had been 'supremely happy as a much-educated woman—not just happy and educated, but happy because educated, able to do what I am cut out to do. I always thank my stars I was born in a century where one got a choice—where all women did not have to be domesticated all the time just because most women want to be domesticated most of the time. It seems I was even luckier than I thought, to catch the brief patch of opportunity between the Victorian age and Sir John Newsom's.'

An interesting and well-informed supplement to Sir John's views, and, at the same time, a qualification of Marghanita Laski's, came three weeks later from a psychologist, Martin

James.[5] Looking at Miss Laski's statement he noted that 'we do not want more womanly women, but more rational women,' for women as politicians and scientists this statement was a truism, but for women as parents and sexual beings it was equally obviously ridiculous. Women's apparent illogicality—so eagerly seized on by the anti-feminists as a proof of male superiority—'is really a devious logic which is a delight both to themselves and their men. It is in fact just as consecutive and sensible in its own way as conceptual rationality based on secondary process and secondary education.' This special feminine logic has however, another point of departure. It is rooted in the logic and rationality of art, dream, illusion and what Freud called 'the primary process' in thinking, which is pictorial and unconscious. It is found in children's thinking and it is 'near to the emotionality which provides much of the colour of life.' Woman as parent, Mr James believed, starts from the assumption that what is good for her baby is good for the country too. The well-being of children is her compass and guide, and when woman as parent is rational instead of intuitive it is a serious matter both for herself and her child.

D. W. Winnicott has usefully expressed this in his *The Child, the Family and the Outside World*, when he says, 'motherhood requires devotion, not cleverness.' To be successful, mothering requires, in fact, 'a life inimical to mental concentration', for it requires devotion to the child's needs and logic not rationality. This favours 'the protective and cow-like state of preoccupation, which, as many a mother laments, overtakes even the cleverest and best educated woman during pregnancy and remains with her while she cares for young children.'

This can be regarded as good sense, as a truism or as a cunning piece of reactionary anti-feminism, according to one's prejudices and predilection. It has nothing to do with the mental abilities or potentialities of women. It describes a temporary state of mind which, given the size of modern British families, is not likely to characterise a woman's life for more than a relatively short period, although many women enjoy these particular years so much that they never really outgrow them, a fact which men can find irritating and puzzling.

There is little evidence that abilities are sex-linked. Girls must therefore inherit talents and aptitudes equally with their brothers, but they may and do show less desire or have less opportunity to cultivate certain of them. In most women ambition is a less powerful driving force than a desire for service and financial rewards less attractive than satisfaction and interest. It is a sad fact that in Britain, although as many girls as boys obtain five or more General Certificate of Education passes at 'O' level, many fewer girls remain at school until the age of eighteen; those leaving at sixteen include many very able girls with seven, eight or more passes. Boys of similar ability almost without exception remain at school and progress to some form of higher education. This is as common in independent and direct-grant schools as it is in maintained schools, so that the influence of home background is not necessarily, as many people believe, one of the reasons for early leaving.

Many, possibly most, girls develop an aversion to school uniform, school discipline or compulsory games, but this is probably not the main reason why they leave school earlier than they should. They do so because they find the school atmosphere impossibly oppressive and they need to escape from it. They decide to marry as early as possible and to experience something of the outside world before they do. The usual sixth-form course can hold few attractions for them. Most girls do not want to study two or three subjects in Advanced-level depth. They would, on the other hand, like to continue a broad general education and then to start new subjects which seem to them relevant to the modern world and to their place in it. The present educational system takes little account of this, and university requirements help to drive them away from school.[6]

Anti-feminists can easily say—and frequently do—that this inability to stay the academic course is merely further evidence of the wastefulness of the higher education of women and girls. What it really proves, however, is the urgent need to develop new courses of an entirely different kind, not necessarily full-time, and not necessarily to be taken in one continuous period.

It has been sensibly suggested that some generalised form of vocational education at the age of sixteen is appropriate to girls and that, at that age, they are prepared to commit themselves to a three-year but not to a five-year course.

Some of the fields which attract women and in which they are badly needed—nursing, teaching the young and the handicapped, social and medical work—have a common core of educational value, whether or not it is followed by the appropriate specialist training for each individual field. At the completion of the initial three-year general course, girls would be qualified for work at a certain level. To become fully qualified they would need to embark on further study or training, taken either at once or at some later date. This further training could be either part-time or full-time, and it would be up-to-date.

A similar system could be worked out for languages, secretarial training, and business studies. Work for a university degree could easily be divided into two parts with the possibility of part two resulting in the granting of a degree, being completed after a break and, if necessary, on a part-time basis. There is no reason why the work for part two should be done during the day. It could just as well be done in the evenings, if universities would reorganise themselves to make the necessary provision. There is now evidence (summarised in Dr Kenneth Soddy's book *Men in Middle Age*) that both men and women can find great satisfaction in learning a new skill in the middle part of their life, when time and energy no longer has to be mainly devoted to looking after children. They may be somewhat slower to learn in their forties than they would have been in their twenties, but they can possess strong motivation and capacity for creative work or study.

The National Union of Students recently (1966) published a report on *Women and Higher Education*. It was concerned—and still is—with the disillusionment felt by many women graduates who find themselves equipped for nothing when they leave the university and wonder why they were there in the first place. The report criticised the present bias in the education of girls towards the arts and the humanities which fails to equip them for professional or highly-skilled work, and recommended that more vocational studies should be introduced into first degree courses.

Parents, school-teachers—always anxious to get as many pupils as possible to the university—and the pupils themselves should be warned in unmistakable terms about the difficulties of indiscriminate higher education. As long as university places for women were limited to dedicated blue stockings who intended to stay in the academic world, there was no serious problem. Teachers and research workers begat teachers and research workers. In the years immediately after the second world war there was something of a fashion for employing young women graduates in journalism, publishing, advertising and various commercial concerns. This unfortunately gave the impression that a degree took a girl halfway up the ladder with no great luck or effort. This is certainly not the present situation, where the demand for women arts graduates with no additional training does not equal the supply. A large number of non-academic girls who slog their way through university would probably be just as happy, if not happier, if they left school at sixteen or eighteen. The same, of course, applies to many non-academic boys, but they do not find the labour market so difficult as the girls at twenty-one, because more firms are willing to engage and train them, reckoning they may have their services for a number of years; the girls, rightly or wrongly, are expected to stay only a short time.

It is easy to wonder why more girls, given the employment situation described above, do not opt for a science-based career. The problem has been investigated by a research group at the London School of Economics.[7] Their report was based on a survey of seventeen schools and eight firms, the aim being to gain information about the attitudes of schoolgirls to science and science-based careers and on the opportunities open to them both at school and in industry. Although they discovered no evidence that girls lack aptitude for scientific subjects, the girls they questioned often mentioned that science was thought to be unfeminine, and this fact certainly influenced their academic performance where science was concerned. Somewhat surprisingly, however, mathematics was chosen as a girl's favourite subject more often than any other, including the traditionally feminine choices of English and modern languages.

Where a school had a large proportion of first-generation grammar-school pupils, the staff found that to these girls and their parents arts subjects represented social advance and freedom, whereas science tended to be thought of as a road back to industry, where the parents were employed, and consequently had a low prestige. Much of this kind of prejudice is based on ignorance of what a scientific career can offer. This is even more true of engineering than it is of science. Rugby College of Engineering Technology has made a special effort to interest more girls in engineering but has found that headmistresses need infinite teaching and persuasion before they are prepared to encourage girls to consider such a career. 'One headmistress,' *The Guardian* found, 'treated the suggestion with a sort of hopeless ignorance; it just wasn't on, whilst another, with more effort to her credit, had not realised that a student could be college based for the purpose of a grant from her LEA, and did not have to be an industrially sponsored student.'[8]

There is considerable disagreement as to whether a mixed school gives girls, and their teachers, a more flexible outlook towards careers and interests. In mixed schools, the chances of a woman securing a headship, or being put in charge of an important department, are not great. Women tend to put an emphasis on different qualities and different kinds of school organisation, and their special contribution to education does not necessarily find an adequate outlet in mixed schools, where the male attitude is likely to win. Miss Margaret Higgison has studied this phenomenon with some care, and believes that among teachers there are certain 'characteristics, insights and methods of organisation' that arise out of the masculine and feminine outlooks on life.[9] Neither is necessarily better than the other and each may suit one sex rather better than the other. It seems to be generally agreed, for instance, that most boys can stand up better than girls to competition and do not suffer so much from being driven. But where pupils are mixed, there should be a fifty-fifty chance of either emphasis prevailing in the school's general policy. The characteristics which Miss Higgison considers 'marks of the feminine outlook' may of course be found in some boys' or mixed schools and be absent from some girls' schools. Four appear to be particularly important:

1 A minimum of 'streaming', positions in form and other badges of competition. There is no streaming at St Paul's or King Edward's, Birmingham, joint winners of the Oxbridge Stakes for 1966.
2 Avoidance of early specialisation.
3 Stress on general and aesthetic subjects, together with the belief that a subject does not have to be publicly examined before it is taken seriously. The Crowther Report commended the girls' schools on the width of their sixth-form courses. 'Headmistresses,' says Miss Higgison, 'wage an unremitting war with male training college principals who demand A levels with everything.'
4 No hierarchy in the staff room. Girls' schools almost always share out sixth-form work among all those able and willing to do it, down to the rawest beginner, whereas in schools with men on the staff it is common to find someone who takes all the sixth-form work and in the rest of the school teaches only top-stream pupils.

There is widespread resentment among women teachers at the practice of appointing male heads to mixed schools, especially when these schools are 'comprehensives', products of the merger of former girls' and boys' schools. The following letter to *The Times Educational Supplement*[10] expresses this:

'I feel that it is time that women rebelled against the deplorable habit of appointing men as heads and deputies of mixed schools. Too many posts of senior mistress are advertised in your columns. Any woman applying for one should be considered as a traitor to her sex. She is only needed to do the unpleasant part of the deputy head's job—the disciplining of the girls—while a man receives the credit. So long as this state of things continues there is no future for the capable woman other than giving up teaching and using her talents in a field where women are considered for their own merit.'

A number of local authorities have countered by saying that they are anxious to appoint women to these responsible positions, but that relatively few women apply and those that do are simply not as good as the men. This also seems to be true in the case of training colleges. In 1966 *The Guardian* published a letter from Mr L. Conneck, Principal of the City of Leeds College of Education.[11]

'In this College of Education where there have always been more women students than men students, the teaching staff is steadily becoming predominantly male. But there is no anti-feminism. All posts are open to women, yet the posts advertised this year (excluding handicraft, which is not expected to attract women) attracted 370 applications from men and only 34 from women.'

This experience was similar to that described in another letter from Mr B. Larwood,[12] a governor of one of the largest mixed colleges in the North West. The college had advertised for a woman as vice-principal, but all the candidates were 'lacking in administrative experience', so it readvertised, this time for a man or a woman, and two women were short-listed with four men. 'I went to the meeting,' said Mr Larwood, 'prepared to fight for a woman candidate should she prove suitable, as I was aware of a certain reluctance within the college to appoint a woman. Both women lacked administrative experience, and during the interview did not impress one regarding their capability of handling awkward men students should the need arise.

Neither appeared to have the stability or the maturity of the men candidates. Consequently, a man was appointed to a post which was intended for a woman. It seems that there are not enough women around of capability and experience. Maybe for biological reasons, in a predominantly male-conditioned society the dice are too heavily loaded against producing many women who are suitable for posts of like responsibility.'

Another, though minor, hierarchical feature of male-dominated schools is anathema to women. Whereas many men teachers seem actually to enjoy addressing the headmaster as 'headmaster' or 'sir'—it gives an old-fashioned public or preparatory school tone to the place—few, if any women would soil their lips with such servility. Hierarchies and their symbols give the majority of women no pleasure at all.

At Oxford and Cambridge the movement to convert more male colleges into mixed colleges has made little progress at the undergraduate level, rather more where postgraduates or Fellows are concerned. In the so-called mixed colleges, however, the women Fellows are, as Miss Margaret Masterman has emphasised, 'only peripheral'.[13] Miss Masterman, Director of Research at the Cambridge Language Research Unit, noted that the Fellows in these colleges had broken taboos by admitting some women, 'but they have never dreamed of granting them true equality of control. The result is that the senior women in "mixed" colleges will never be educated by sufficient opportunity to hold office; and the junior women, observing the non-essential positions held by their seniors, will have no inducement to do anything but study for three years in the college, and then leave it.'

Miss Masterman quoted a selection of choice statements which she had recently heard. One came from an Anglican bishop: 'But I am a liberal: I would always prefer a first-rate woman to a third-rate man.' Another occurred in a conversation between an old-established women's group and a raw new men's group, who were discussing 'mixing'. The head woman asked how the men would consider distributing the offices, to which the head man replied: 'Oh, we would raise no objection to having one woman vice-president.' The officer of a men's college said they wanted to become mixed, but were unable to discover a suitable woman to make a Fellow. When asked 'Well, would you ever consider having her later as your President?' his answer was: 'Of course not; anything like that would be quite out of the question.' Miss Masterman's conclusion was that while this remained the attitude of the men in a mixed college it was clear that something was inherently wrong with the mixture and that there was therefore still something to be said for single-sex colleges.

Many teachers with experience of both boarding and day schools consider that, whatever advantages a boarding education may have for boys, there is little to be said in its favour for the majority of girls. There are, of course, boarding schools and boarding schools, and there have been many changes, mostly for the better, in the past twenty years. One wonders, even so, how many girls today are presented at boarding school with conditions not unlike those they suffered at Cheltenham Ladies' College during the late 1940s. Here was, and is, a high-prestige establishment, with some of the finest academic results in the country. Yet, 'the school's general policy', an ex-pupil recalled ten years later, 'was to treat us all as mentally defective delinquents, who at the least "little dust of praise" would become unmanageable. Dormitory don'ts were unlimited: no girl could enter another's cubicle, no hair curlers, food, books, pills or cosmetics could be taken there. Parcels from home had to be opened in the presence of the staff and the contents were scrutinised and sometimes confiscated. Nothing was sacrosanct, nowhere our own. Lockers and drawers were regularly inspected for neatness and contraband. "Men" were tacitly admitted by the authorities as an extramural menace, whose existence should be acknowledged only when unavoidable. We were never allowed out singly because of them, and could shop only in a restricted section of the town—and that but rarely. Envelopes waiting to be posted—it was a crime to approach a pillar-box ourselves—were inspected, and anything addressed to a man, other than father or brother, had to be checked against the writer's list of permitted correspondents.'[14]

Katharine Whitehorn has similar memories of another prestige boarding school, Roedean. The establishment of Roedean, as of Cheltenham, was, among other things, a triumph of nineteenth-century feminism. It gave girls from professional families the same kind of schooling as their brothers. Miss Whitehorn's main reason for disliking it was the sense of captivity it gave her. Never at any point in the twenty-four hours was a girl free—'free of the school, of the other girls' opinions, of the stiff-upper-lip-ruling that prevented some girls who were just as unhappy as I was even telling their parents they were miserable.' She failed to see any point at all in toughening up girls like this. The boys' public schools, for which she holds no special brief anyway, appeared to make some sort of sociological sense. 'You take the youths at puberty away from their mothers' softening influence, you give them tough exercises to make them strong warriors and to keep their minds off sex, you give them a glorious games hierarchy to fight their way up and at the end of it they have been through an initiation. They have no doubt of their identity as British, upper-middle-class, and male. But how can you possibly apply the same tribal techniques to girls, who have the opposite things to learn?'

As a classic example of the irrelevance of these 'tribal techniques', she mentioned the boarding-school attitude to illness. 'One house matron is tough; no good going to her because you felt too frightful for cricket practice before breakfast. Another is more sympathetic—and the chances are she is regarded as "soft". Yet which are women supposed to be—good at comforting the sick, or good at spotting malingerers, like a sergeant-major?'

The philosophy underlying the boarding education of girls appears to be, to say the least of it, ill-considered. It is consequently curious that much the most intelligent and thoroughgoing recent investigation of the public schools, that carried out by Dr Royston Lambert, should have presented its findings so overwhelmingly in terms of boys.[15] Much of what he has to report is as applicable to girls as it is to boys; an excellent example is the section in which he is discussing what he calls 'Loyalty in a Closed Society'. Dr Lambert, who was not at a public school himself, notes that since he came away from home at the tender age of eight or thereabouts, 'to live continuously and without privacy under the savage scrutiny of an all-male society, the public school boy has had to protect the most deeply vulnerable areas of self from hurt; to conceal emotions, restrain expressions of tender feelings or certain kinds of imagination.

'The artificial nature of boarding itself removes from boys some of the common situations in outside experience where deep emotions are aroused and have to be faced continually. In addition, relations with adults in the boarding community are meant to be objective or non-affective in nature. Indeed this is where, it is claimed, they score over the emotionally cluttered relationships of parent-child. The accepted tone is, therefore, one of affective neutrality; one which inhibits expression of the inner self, or emotions, spontaneity or extreme reactions. It encourages instead responses which are protectively rational, considered, and moderate, unrevealing of embarrassing personal forces. In a single-sex school deeply affective relations between pupils cannot be approved. Access to affective relations outside—parents, relatives, the other sex—is curtailed. For many they cease to be an everyday reality with profound consequences for later life. The gregarious life and pupil and staff norms make repression the done thing; displays of emotion, tender feelings of extreme enthusiasm or types of imagination are severely and sometimes cruelly controlled by the pupil society. Or they are deprecated as unmanly or even vulgar by the staff. A public self operates all the time. The private self partially atrophies or is deeply submerged.'

Little of this is not equally applicable to girls. An aspect of boarding-school conditioning which lay outside Dr Lambert's field of investigation is the extent to which the years spent away from her family, and especially her father, cause emotional unbalance which makes it more difficult for a girl to choose a suitable husband in the first place and to settle down easily to marriage afterwards. In this and in other matters, the relationship between the education girls receive and the quality and satisfaction of their lives afterwards has been very inadequately studied. Educationally, women are still living in the backwash of militant feminism.

THREE

Women in Employment

What paid work do women actually do and how many of them work at all?

A survey undertaken for the TUC's Women's Advisory Committee and published in April 1965 shows that in Britain the proportion of women in the labour force has been very stable. It was 30.7 per cent in 1851 and 33.9 per cent in 1963. In 1851 a third of all women workers were domestic servants. In 1931 this had fallen to 26 per cent (1,332,000+ 140,000 charwomen) and by 1963 to 10 per cent (217,000 in private domestic service, 384,000 in hotels and catering).

The survey also reveals a change in the age pattern of working women. The number of women under twenty-five who work has dropped, while the number between twenty-five and forty-four has remained stable and that above forty-four has risen sharply. While the total number of working women in 1911 was less than two-thirds of the present number, more women under twenty-five were at work than are now. But the proportion of working women over forty-four has gone up from one-seventh to one-third. The proportion of married women in the work force has also risen. Fifty years ago only one married woman in ten worked away from home, whereas today one in three does so.

Notes to this chapter are on page 172

Women in Employment

Single and married women at work, 1911-63

	1911	1953	1963
	%	%	%
Single	86	55	47
Married	14	45	53

Proportion of women workers in each 100 of their age group, 1953 and 1963

	1953	1963
Under 20	77.1	71.5
20-24	66.2	62.2
25-34	38.6	38.4
35-44	37.6	45.4
45-54	37.0	47.0
55-59	29.9	39.7
60-64	15.4	21.3
65 and over	3.8	4.8
	35.6	38.7

Women employees as a percentage of total labour force by region, 1953-63

	1953	1963
Scotland	10.2	9.7
Northumberland, Cumberland, Durham	5.0	5.1
Lancashire	15.3	13.7
Wales	3.5	3.6
Midlands and rest of North-East	24.5	24.6
Gloucestershire and South-West	4.8	5.5
South and East	9.5	11.0
South-East	27.2	26.8
Total, all regions	24.5	24.6

At the time of writing, the latest available figures (May 1967) compiled by the Ministry of Labour showed that there were nearly 8,000,000 working women in the United Kingdom. This figure represented 37.5 per cent of the women aged fifteen and over, or just over 32 per cent of the total active labour force in the country.

Of the total of 8,000,000 24.3 per cent worked part-time and only 2.7 per cent were in managerial positions of any kind. Only 0.7 per cent were members of the recognised professions. More than 50 per cent were married, compared with only 10 per cent in 1941. Today it is estimated that at least 40 per cent of married women aged thirty-five and over go out to work and by 1972 it is expected that more than 5,000,000 married women will have jobs of some kind outside the home, although this estimate may be upset by technological changes.

Although only 29 per cent of the labour force, women account for 37 per cent of the unskilled or skilled manual workers. They represent only 11.7 per cent of members of the professions, including teaching where they predominate, and comprise 16 per cent of managers. Only 2.2 per cent of the female population of the appropriate age group are students, against 9.6 per cent of males.

In certain industries women far outnumber men. They are dominant in the distributive trades, the professional and scientific industries and in insurance, banking and finance, mostly at the lower levels. At the unskilled level, women tend to do the work that men, or at any rate British men with white skins, refuse—in the domestic or catering trades, and routine conveyor-line work in breweries, cosmetic factories and the like. For certain kinds of industrial jobs women are more suitable: this is particularly true in electronics, where men's hands lack the necessary dexterity.

A quantitative answer of a different kind has also been given by the Ministry of Labour.[1] The Minstry's analysis uses A to indicate the percentage of married women in the total labour force and B the percentage of unmarried women:

Under 20		20-39		40-59		60+	
A 1	B 17	A 21	B 16	A 28	B 11	A 3	B 3

The figures for manufacturing and for the service industries are not significantly different.

Again for all industries and services, the percentage of married women, expressed as a percentage of all female employees, is:

Age	15-19	3.6
	20-24	32.9
	25-34	66.5
	35-44	78.2
	45-54	71.6
	55-59	59.4
	60+	50.0

The proportion of female employees within the total varies regionally, being highest in the north and lowest in the south-east, with a national average of 18 per cent.

The Ministry report notes that for female employees under twenty, the proportion in all industries and services rose from 17 per cent in 1962 to 18 per cent in 1963. For the age groups twenty to thirty-nine and sixty and over there were no changes in comparison with 1962 (37 per cent and 6 per cent respectively), but the proportion aged forty—fifty-nine fell by 1 per cent to 39 per cent. The employment group with the highest proportion of women under twenty was insurance, banking and finance, with 31 per cent. The clothing and footwear and distributive trades each had 20 per cent, showing increases of 1 per cent and 2 per cent respectively compared with 1962. Professional and scientific services had 8 per cent and public administration 11 per cent in this age group.

The Ministry's approach is of course entirely and properly objective; it has no attitude toward the proportion of women employed in a particular industry. When a crusading body turns its attention to statistics the results inevitably give a different impression. In 1964 the National Council for Civil Liberties published a report with the tendentious title *Discrimination against Women,* showing the numbers of women active in various professions. The main conclusions were as follows:

Law: 103 women practising barristers out of a total of 2,073. Only four were QCs. There had never at that time been a woman judge in the High Court. There was one woman judge in the County Courts, one woman sheriff in Scotland, and one recorder (Burnley). Just over 400 women were practising solicitors, out of a total of 20,250.

Accountants: 11,000 chartered accountants, 82 of them women.

BBC: When the survey was made, women held six of the 150 'top' jobs in the BBC. Of the executive posts, women occupied less than one-third and they appeared more frequently as assistants than as principals.

Journalism: About 2,000 women among the 18,000 members of the National Union of Journalists. There had never been a woman editor of a daily newspaper and even among the magazines which cater especially for women the majority of editors had been male.

Medicine: 17 per cent of those on the Medical Register were women. At the consultant level women represented between only 3 and 4 per cent of the total and even in local health authority work the percentage of senior posts they occupied was small.

Taking all medical students in all schools, just under 24 per cent were women and about 400 qualified each year. Figures for six London medical schools given by Lord Taylor in the House of Lords on 10 March 1964 showed that 344 out of 7,625 male applicants (one in every twenty-two) were successful, and only 90 out of 3,360 women (one in thirty-seven). In one of the most popular schools, acceptance was one in forty-three for men and one in seventy-three for women.

Dentists: 1,446 women out of 16,279 on the Register.

Architects: About 700 women were working as architects, against 16,300 men.

Civil Service: In the Civil Service as a whole there were 189 women in the Administrative class out of a total of 2,482; in the Foreign Service there were 23 out of 750. In the Executive class there were 358 women in the grades of Senior Executive Officer and above, out of a total of 4,326, and 598 out of 19,003 of equivalent level in the Professional, Scientific and Upper Technical classes. In the Civil Service as a whole (excluding manual grades) there were more than 600,000 workers, and about one-third of these were women, including 30,000 typists.

The vast majority of women, therefore, were in the lower-paid grades, and only a tiny fraction (about 0.3 per cent) in the Administrative class, whose main function is the key job of advising ministers on the formation of policy.

Finance and commerce: Of 40,574 members of the Institute of Directors, only 850 were women. There were few in the big companies and none at all in the biggest. There were also very few in managerial posts in the business world and even fewer at company-secretary level. Out of 6,000 Fellows of the Chartered Institute of Secretaries, only 79 were women.

Taking a more general look at the position of women in public life, *Discrimination against Women* discovered that in 1964 there were 25 women among the 630 MPs in the Parliament just dissolved and 8 life peeresses. The last cabinet did not include a woman. In the forty-six years that women have been eligible to sit in the Commons, there have been only three women cabinet ministers.

There were at that time no women on the National Coal Board, Port of London Authority, Bank of England, British Overseas Airways Corporation, British European Airways, Central Electricity Board, Gas Council, UK Atomic Energy Authority and British Transport Commission.

On local councils women held a much larger proportion of the seats than in the Commons, but only in London, in some of the larger cities and in a few counties and boroughs in the southern half of the country could they be found in appreciable numbers.

The controversy over the alleged lack of opportunities for professional women has inevitably been especially bitter, because this is the type of woman most likely to feel frustrated if she believes that her talents, education and training are being wasted, under-used or under-paid.

A curious feature of the employment situation among professional women is that salaries have remained very low in the seriously short-staffed professions. The normal result of too many jobs chasing too few people has not occurred and one wonders how much worse the position must get before salaries begin to rise dramatically. Working conditions are of course as important as salaries. In September 1964 the *Nursing Mirror* forecast that the nursing situation would be out of hand by 1970 and wondered if any remedy could be found in time. 'The record of the profession makes one doubt it. A minority of matrons willing to tailor the job to the applicant, a minimum number of full-time nurses willing to accept part-time married nurses as friends and colleagues, only a handful of crèches for working mothers' children—these are hardly indicative of a profession alive to a situation growing more desperate every year and likely to be catastrophic by 1970.'

Two years later Viola Klein published disturbing figures for a whole range of professions in which women are all-important.[2] Almoners, for instance, estimated a 65 per cent shortage, dieticians a 42 per cent shortage, librarians a 50 per cent shortage, occupational therapists a 24 per cent shortage, orthopticians a $33\frac{1}{3}$ per cent shortage, and radiographers a 21 per cent shortage.

In the professions dominated by men, nearly all employers, when pressed, will deny that they are prejudiced against appointing women to senior positions, just as they will deny that they operate a colour bar. Their answer is usually that for some strange and regrettable reason the right kind of women do not seem to be available for the big jobs they have to offer. The BBC has come under heavy fire for many years for its supposedly anti-feminist bias. Early in 1962, for instance, Dame Thelma Cazalet Keir, a former Governor of the BBC, wrote to *The Times*[3] to point out that according to the information contained in the latest edition of the *BBC Handbook*, out of 150 top jobs only four were held by women.

These four included, 'not unnaturally', the Head of Wardrobe and the Head of Women's Programmes. In an organisation like the BBC which had given women and men equal pay since 1926 this seemed strangely backward and way behind even the Civil Service, which had only recently implemented equal pay and yet had a number of women in very important positions. In reply, the BBC's Director of Administration, Mr J. H. Arkell, drew attention[4] to an article published three years earlier in *The Times*,[5] which praised the BBC for its absence of anti-feminism: 'Vacancies are advertised and filled,' said the article, 'according to ability and merit without relation to sex. Here is a community where women compete with men on as nearly equal terms as they are likely to find anywhere in the workaday world. They perform a richly varied assortment of duties.' The position, said Mr Arkell, was still broadly the same.

Mrs Mary Adams, who had had a long and distinguished career with the BBC, continued the correspondence in support of Mrs Cazalet Keir. Women were not in the top jobs at the BBC. The reason was, as always and everywhere, 'that men in top jobs have clubs, not babies, have time to play Parkinson instead of visiting the hairdresser'. Women 'are handicapped in the rat race. But perhaps with half an eye on the biology of eternity, they aren't even trying to win.'[6] Sir John Reith, she recalled, had recruited senior women in the twenties. In the thirties, however, 'professionalism set in and kept women out. During the war women sweated in the basement equally with men, leaving afterwards disillusioned, to return to their families and other jobs. Today, the women who came in the fifties are too inexperienced for the burden of policy responsibilities.'

Mrs Cazalet Keir compared the BBC unfavourably with the Civil Service in the number of women each employed in important posts. In 1966, on the occasion of the appointment of Mrs Eirene White as the first woman to be Minister of State for Foreign Affairs, the Foreign Office took the opportunity to shoot down the myth that it is anti-feminist. It revealed that two heads of department, two assistant heads of department and one legal adviser in its labyrinthine palace were women. Abroad, the score was one counsellor, one consul-general, four women in charge of consulates, and a considerable number of seconds-in-command in consulates.

In the same year, Sir William Haley appointed a woman as assistant city editor. He announced that he had a high opinion of women as journalists and that during his own reign in Printing House Square their numbers had increased, although still not up to what he had known on the *Manchester Guardian*.[7] He was sure that *The Times* would have more women working on it in the years to come, 'partly because it will have more news and features of interest to women, partly because there will be an increase, on all newspapers, in the employment of women journalists as a reflection of what is happening in society at large. The bulkheads between the sexes, in terms of what women do, what they are allowed to do, what they insist on doing, how they are treated in terms of jobs, are fortunately breaking down.'

Mr Donald McLachlan, formerly editor of the *Sunday Telegraph*, has said that the appointment of a woman editor for a national daily or Sunday newspaper is long overdue.[8] 'Male prejudice apart, I can see no reason why it should not happen. If it is argued that very few women have ever written with skill and authority on politics, the answer is that no editor need be a skilled political writer—indeed few editors are. A woman editor could direct a male political staff every bit as well as a man editor directs a female features staff; indeed, she might rescue the subject from some of the parochial triviality that now pervades it.

'As things are, women may climb well over halfway up the professional tree and then get stranded on a branch called the women's pages or women's features, or write a regular column of views like Anne Scott-James or Monica Furlong, perhaps the most agreeable consummation of all. Yet circulation-wise, and from the advertisers' point of view, they are decisive figures, helping to form as they do consumers' fashions not only in clothes, cosmetics and hair-dos, but also in interior decoration, cooking, health, child-rearing and holidays—to say nothing of morals and what used to be private intimacies of married and unmarried life.

'As for stamina—the ability to survive long hours, intense competition, hurried writing, bullying by telephone and elbowing of cameramen—I know of few ordeals faced by the male reporter to compare with the scrimmage at the Paris and Rome fashion shows.'

Editors apart, the best record for employing women in national journalism is probably that of the *Economist*. Of its full-time, London-based editorial staff of forty, thirteen are what it calls 'responsible women'.[9]

The banks, formerly exclusively male preserves on their higher levels, have weakened a little since 1945. Barclays now have four women to manage branches and one inspector. In February 1967, the Bank of England appointed Miss A. P. M. Maunsell as Deputy Chief of Establishments, the highest post a woman has yet held with the Bank. Miss Maunsell has spent her whole career with the Bank of England, joining it in 1936 when aged eighteen. 'The Bank claims that its staff is now fully integrated and that it is possible for a woman to rise to the highest position. Many women hold responsible administrative posts which a few years ago would have been reserved for men.'[10]

Industrial management has probably been the most difficult field for women to break into, even at a trainee level. Unilever, Marks & Spencer, Ford and ICI, however, all recruit women for management training now. Ford believes that trainees pay off in two years, its personnel manager being quoted as having said, 'If women leave then to have babies, it's no different from our point of view to a finance man leaving for a higher salary.'[11]

Michael Fogarty, consultant to Political & Economic Planning on a project run jointly by it and the Tavistock Institute to consider the use of women in senior posts, believes that, like the arts men, the women graduates are going to find it easier to beat a path in an industrial and commercial world increasingly dominated by control systems if they are prepared to acquire appropriate skills. One of the most important of these skills is numeracy. Professor Fogarty points out that the existence of new specialities makes it much easier for women to spot the coming roads to the top. Management used to be a vague concept, but now that it is increasingly dependent on specialisation, a woman finds fewer barriers if she has a marketable qualification.

He believes that the return of women to work after a break for child-rearing may have to be treated on exactly the same basis as the entry of ex-officers, with similar training programmes. For anyone coming into industry at over fifty there will only be specialist or personnel jobs. 'At forty to forty-five, there's not enough time to get into a senior job, but if one can get restarted before thirty-five there is time to get into the normal promotional scheme.'

Professor Fogarty's full report has not yet been published, but some of its conclusions have already emerged. 'One of the most alarming is that nobody wants more able people—even if they were all men. While there is employment for the young graduates up to thirty-five and for the £10,000 a year man, there is a shortage of "top" posts in between.' He even quotes one university appointments board as 'selling' its women graduates along the lines: 'Isn't it wonderful, they won't be around in twenty years' time.'[12]

The difficulty for most women with management ambitions is to find a firm that will allow them to get started. Though few firms will admit to having a definite policy not to send women on management courses, some say frankly that in their management development plans they aim to take women about two-thirds of the way up the ladder and no further.

Portsmouth College of Technology has had much experience in running management courses. The Principal, Dr W. Davey, has said that women who are aware of their firm's policy to stop them rising beyond a certain level 'will obviously not give the same single-minded attention to their career in the firm.'[13]

He mentioned a firm with a payroll of 60,000 which had

named only six women among the 600 employees selected as likely to be worth training for management. Other people concerned with management training have had the same experience. Not a single British firm has sent a woman to the Oxford University Business Summer School for bright young executives. The average age of those attending is thirty-two and the selection standards are high. The School would like to have women, but none come. The proportion of women attending leading management training courses in the United States is also low.

The Vitamins Group and Burroughs Wellcome have an exceptionally enlightened policy for employing women in management. At Vitamins, which has two women on the board, one-eighth of the senior staff are women—the proportion is even higher where technical posts are concerned—and whenever suitable courses come up at the British Institute of Management or elsewhere it is taken for granted that the women will be as eligible for nomination as the men. The group has equal pay for women from clerical level right up to the top. At Burroughs Wellcome, one in every five monthly-paid staff is a woman; having found that women compare well, and mix well, with men on courses, the firm regularly sends them in considerable numbers for training in work-study, industrial supervision, personnel and welfare work and senior management—many of these courses being run within the organisation.

It will clearly be a long time before it is regarded as normal for girls to take up an engineering, scientific or technical career. As the *Economist* has pointed out,[14] 'there are real problems aside from the unreal ones of male ignorance and prejudice. There can be no waving of a magic wand that would elicit in the British polity a group as worthy as those famous and burly Russian lady engineers whom western man, however enlightened, understandably regards with a certain awe. Anyone who wants to become a technologist or a scientist has to make his or her choice pretty early in life; family attitudes, and the entire social ethos of a nation, and at least three generations of parents, teachers and pupils must be changed before it becomes regarded as normal for a young girl to aim at a career in industry.

'It should be suggested to employers that, in the long run, paying women much less than men is a false economy; for if the pool of talent for responsible jobs is artificially small because the attraction of those jobs to women is minimised by low pay,[15] this must mean that the increasingly inadequate pool of (almost exclusively male) labour trained for those jobs will be able to demand disproportionately high salaries.' One further point that British industry might consider is that educated British women usually prefer to stay in Britain.

At present, however, industry has too few attractions for most educated women. The 1965 report of the appointments board for Newcastle & Durham Universities makes this all too clear. After emphasising that many more women than men graduates stated that their picture of industry was 'wholly uncongenial', the Appointments Officer continued, 'This is partly a picture of dark, satanic mills, but more important, partly also of a tough masculine world into which women are allowed to intrude only on sufferance and to tackle relatively menial tasks often well below their intellectual capacity. The final obstacle to the woman student who is genuinely interested in getting into industry is often the discovery that teaching is, for her, financially more attractive. At the moment, there is little or no incentive to industry to concern itself with this situation.'

In the 1960s women's principal economic grievances have been: unequal pay, barriers to mothers working, closed or supposedly closed professions, barriers to promotion and responsible posts, lack of apprenticeship and retraining schemes, and tax and national insurance anomalies.

The Treaty of Rome established the principle of equal pay for equal work, but within the European Economic Community none of the member states (including France, mainly at whose insistence Article 119 was inserted in the Treaty) has fully implemented the principle. Considerable progress has been made in most of the EEC states, and women's wages have risen faster than those of men in recent years, but, in Europe as in America, there is still a long way to go before the objective is finally reached. In Britain, after seventy years of argument and pious resolutions, the process has hardly begun. At the Trades Union Congress in 1965, for instance, a motion on equal pay for women produced the usual basic rallying cry of 'sweated labour' and Congress responded approvingly as it always does. In moving the motion, Mr D. E. Newton of the National Union of Tailors & Garment Workers said, with perfect accuracy, that without women workers his own industry would collapse, but they were, even so, still often used as a source of cheap labour. For all industry, the average earnings for women, on the April 1965 figures, were only £9 4s 0d compared with £18 18s 0d for the men, and if the hourly earnings rate was available it would give an even worse picture. One should also take into account the added strain that many women had to face as a result of having to manage a home as well as take employment.

'We may have abolished starvation,' Mr Newton told Congress, 'but we have not abolished sweating, and it is mainly the women who are being sweated.' A policy of inequality between men's and women's wages was a bad policy, he said and the Government ought to show a serious intention of dealing with the problem. 'We should be very glad if they would deal with it in the next four months.' But of course it did not, any more than it had during the past half-century and more; Government, TUC and individual trade unions have always given the matter a very low priority. The craft unions in particular have had a reactionary policy towards women workers, representing the extreme conservatism of the traditional type of British working man—though few trade unions would admit this in public.

A notable exception to this general reticence is the National Union of School Masters, which has a strongly anti-feminist philosophy. The Union's 1966 annual conference debated a motion to increase the salaries of men teachers and leave those of women at their existing level.[16] Supporting this, a member of the executive said, 'The economy must distinguish between the bird of passage and the salt of the earth. We should not be devoting our resources to the shifting sands of mercenaries.' Few trade-union spokesmen would have dared to be so blunt. The villain has usually to be the employer.

'Some employers had a Victorian attitude towards women and did not believe in equal pay for equal work,' the Royal Commission on Trade Unions & Employers' Associations was told on 2 March 1966. Mrs J. Mineau, an official of the National Federation of Professional Workers, said that at least two general managers had told her they did not believe in equal pay for women, and she claimed to have evidence that many others supported the same policy. 'They say the basis of their argument is that a man has a wife and children to support and they use the teachers as an example. They claim a woman teacher can go on continental holidays while a married man can hardly afford to go to Southend.'

This indefensible form of reasoning is convenient for employers, both private and public, because it allows them to get their women workers cheaply, knowing that the male-controlled trade unions and their members will not object. The membership figures show how relatively unimportant women are to the trade unions, particularly to the politically powerful unions. During 1965-6, the AEU for example increased its women's membership by 9,091. It had, on 5 April 1966, 100,000 women in a total membership of 1.1 million. During the past five years its women's membership increased by 22,000 or 30 per cent; about 15,500 of these were recruited in the past two years. To help cater for their special interests the union in 1966 appointed a woman technical assistant at its headquarters, but this remains a junior post, ranking low in the AEU hierarchy. A woman's election in March 1968 as a district president of the Amalgamated Union of Engineering & Foundry Workers was something of a breakthrough in heavy industry.

In August 1967, the Minister of Labour set up a tripartite

working party with the Confederation of British Industry and the TUC to investigate the whole question of equal pay for women. After nine months, the working party had failed to agree on any of the four things it was asked to examine—definition, cost, methods of implementation and timing.[17] The eventual cost to industry, given the same number of women to be employed, would be large and the employers would naturally do much to avoid having to pay it. It was in fact estimated that it would add about 2½ to 6½ per cent to the national wage bill. The official view apparently was that it would be from 3 to 5 per cent, according to how it was operated, but the employers thought it would be 6 per cent, which would mean a cost to industry of £1,200,000,000 a year, without any consequential increase in productivity, unless of course one result of higher wages was to reduce the number of women employed and give those who remained more advanced machinery to operate.

Perhaps the most intractable conflict of view was over definition. The employers wanted to use that definition in Article 119 of the Treaty of Rome which can be summarised as equal pay 'for the same work'; the TUC, on the other hand, wanted ratification of ILO Convention No 100 which provides for equal pay for work of equal value. This would mean not only raising the pay of women doing men's work but also of women doing 'women's work' if this could be shown to be of equal value to that of men earning more. But that in turn might imply paying all men the same for work of equal value, which would involve nothing less than a national job-evaluation programme. On the other side the Treaty of Rome definition has been criticised on the grounds that employers would more and more segregate men and women in different jobs, so that, from the women's point of view, the cure might turn out to be worse than the disease.

As for timing, the CBI thought that talking about equal pay was unreal in present economic circumstances, and that Britain should wait to see whether it would enter the European Common Market. The TUC representatives felt that there ought to be at the very least a joint statement that the time has come to make a beginning, leaving the rest to collective bargaining.

The TUC established its own working party on equal pay for women, after the failure of the tripartite working party to agree. It completed its report in July 1967 and this was heatedly discussed at the Trades Union Congress in September. On behalf of the Association of Scientific Workers, Mrs J. Hunt said that 'precisely nothing' had been achieved during the past year and blamed the General Council and the Government for giving way to the delaying tactics of the employers. Miss M. Leak, of the National Union of Tailors & Garment Workers, asked Congress what it had to be afraid of. 'Surely not women? If you get the rate for the job, you should see that the lady next to you does as well.' Mr L. M. Bedford, the chairman of this union, told its annual conference in July 1967, 'If equal pay would cost the nation £1,200,000,000 a year, as had been stated, then the women of Britain had been underpaid by that amount.'[18]

The weakness of this appeal to reason is that it ignores the whole question of supply and demand. Women workers are not likely to receive fair treatment so long as enough of them come forward to take the jobs offered at the present low wages, and they will do this so long as they regard their work as only temporary and refuse to acquire real skills. Employers, quite naturally, pay what they need to pay and no more. A great deal of the unskilled and semi-skilled industrial work now being done by women will be automated during the next ten years. The faster wages for women go up, the sooner automation is likely to replace them altogether, a fact of which all parties, except perhaps the women themselves, are aware. This is one reason why most professional women have already won the battle for equal pay. They are not, in general, a temporary substitute for automated machinery.

It seems to be generally agreed that no real progress is being made towards the goal of equal pay because both the employer and the Government—which also happens itself to employ a considerable number of women—are terrified by guesses at the cost. In order to remove the guesswork and at the same time, one hopes, the terrors, a pilot study was started in February 1968 jointly by the Trades Union Congress and the Confederation of British Industry. The researchers are confining their attention to the cost of 'equal pay for work of equal value', although that is often likely to be difficult to define. The latest CBI estimate is that to make this concession would add about 6 per cent to the national wage bill.

In December 1967, just before the pilot study began, the Joint Parliamentary Secretary at the Ministry of Labour, Mr Roy Hattersley, said that the Government was committed to the principle of equal pay. He added, however, in phrases hallowed by years of repetition, that 'in the present economic circumstances it was not possible to take immediate steps to give full implementation to the principle'.[19] Needless to say, 'the Government was anxious to take action to be ready to implement the principle when circumstances were more favourable', and, in an unusually rash and optimistic mood, Mr Hattersley said he would look at existing wage legislation to see if any alterations would be needed if the impossible were to happen and Britain were to be allowed to join the Common Market.

Meanwhile it may be noted that one of the longest and bitterest strikes in recent British industrial history, at Robert-Arundel, Stockport, was caused primarily by this American-based company taking on women instead of men to do a particular job. The Amalgamated Engineering Union objected to this, and blacklisted the factory. The AEU might well have attempted to answer two fundamental questions: why should women join a union which, in effect, guarantees them unequal pay for equal work? And why, since under present conditions women workers in Britain are cheaper to hire, should an employer not take on equal labour at lower rates of pay? But the union restricted itself to telling the country and Robert-Arundel that it was taking a stand on a matter of principle, the principle apparently being that women must always take second place in the labour market.

Although the CBI was not in favour of giving women equal pay, one of its working parties' reports has declared support for ending the existing restrictions on women's employment in factories, including those on working at night[20] which were first introduced in 1844, mainly for moral reasons. It also advocates equalisation of retirement ages for men and women, which would mean raising the retirement age for women from sixty to sixty-five. The report points out that restrictions on women factory workers' hours have become particularly irksome with the spread of shift working. Under the Factories Act women are coupled with young persons in a section limiting their hours to nine in any day, and forty-eight in a week, and stating that they shall not start work earlier than 7.0 am or finish after 8.0 pm; overtime is also restricted. There are no comparable restrictions on non-factory employment.

It is easy to illustrate the gross exploitation which is still normal outside factories. On 7 December 1964 the *Evening Standard* contained the following large display advertisement:

> SECRETARY
> EXTRAORDINARY
>
> We are a leading City firm. We seek a top flight woman secretary, strong enough to cope with a variety of exacting work.
>
> She will have two very high level bosses who are busy and (at times) difficult. Sometimes there are conflicting pressures. Besides complete competence in shorthand and typing we require fluency in French. The job will never be dull. The right woman is unlikely to be under 35 or over 45 and she must put her job first.
>
> Conditions are excellent and salary will be in £1,000 pa region.
>
> Who comes forward?
>
> Apply in complete confidence to Box 3523. *Evening Standard*.

The paragon this firm hoped to find would really be a

personal assistant and a secretary in one. If the post had been designated as that of personal assistant, it would almost certainly have been filled by a man, paid something like £2,000 a year.

In an article in the *FBI Review* for August 1963, Mr A. J. M. Sykes, Head of the Department of Management Studies at the Scottish College of Commerce, Glasgow, argued that the industrial and commercial executive was seriously overloaded and that only the personal assistant could solve the problem. 'Given proper training of personal assistants,' he wrote, 'and willingness by executives to make proper use of them, they can be used to relieve executives of much detailed work. In addition, they can, in many cases, do thoroughly many jobs which at present are the responsibility of executives, but which the latter, owing to pressure of work, neglect, or perform only perfunctorily. The jobs which can be, and are, done by personal assistants in order to save executive time are summarised below.'

I duly wrote to Mr Sykes asking if the upgrading of the personal assistant might not be likely to result in the downgrading of the personal secretary, and suggested that a really good secretary already carried out many of the duties which Mr Sykes had in mind for the personal assistant, particularly in preparing abstracts, gathering information, screening visitors and telephoners, and sifting mail. Would not a little less of it's-a-man's-world in managerial circles, and a good deal more willingness to make fuller, better-paid and more imaginative use of the feminine talent already at their disposal, help to find at least part of the solution to the problem?

In his courteous and detailed reply, Mr Sykes said: 'I would agree with your main point that a good female secretary does most of the jobs I lay down for the personal assistant. However, it is a complicated business. There is always a case for the specialist PA trained in economics or statistics. There is also the fact that many firms are prejudiced against allowing a good secretary the full authority of a PA. I remember one very senior man with a remarkable secretary who tried time after time to get his Board to give her the status she deserved but quite unsuccessfully. They said, quite rightly, that the male managers in the firm would have raised hell about it . . . A lot of use is made of secretaries as PA's but prejudice among senior managers, or fear of prejudice among their staffs, leads to a reluctance to give them proper recognition.'

In February 1967, a Civil Service typist was convicted under the Official Secrets Act and sent to prison. The case drew attention to the difficulty girls in London had to make ends meet, if they came from the provinces or from abroad, and had to live entirely on their earnings. Girls getting £10 to £12 a week were commonly paying £5 10s to £6 a week for rent alone. Their rapid changes of jobs as they seek to earn a few shillings more mean that they have little chance to make real friends. The combination of poverty and loneliness makes some of them desperate for friendship and kindness, too ready to clutch at straws. This can easily lead to them agreeing to sell any employer's secrets they can find, whether Government or industrial.

One girl employed in the Civil Service told *The Guardian*: 'It's unrealistic to expect anyone to manage on £11 a week in London nowadays. It leaves the girls open to temptations and the situation where they will go out with any man, no matter how undesirable the circle he moves in, simply to get a free meal.'[21] The problem is a difficult one. Some of the £10-£12 girls are simply not worth any more to their employers. Such low earners are usually too young to be living more or less friendless in London.

One can argue as to how many girls working in the Civil Service could reasonably consider themselves skilled. Experienced secretaries and shorthand-typists certainly could. They have undergone a substantial course of training in order to acquire saleable skills and they deserve to be paid accordingly. Much routine Civil Service work is of a much lower order, however, and is as easily learnt as assembly work or packing in a factory; some of it is in process of disappearing altogether as the computer takes over. The productivity of a large proportion of both the men and the women employed in Government departments and by local authorities is still low, by modern standards, and this is the main reason why they are badly paid. Their work is not organised with sufficient efficiency to allow them to earn a modern salary. Their economic weakness, as with people in many other occupations, is that there are simply too many of them. The cake has to be shared out among too many people.

Unskilled workers of either sex have always been vulnerable. They are particularly so today, when Britain is becoming increasingly cost-conscious and when the trend is either to use machines or if the workers show signs of pricing themselves and their employers out of the market, to scrap the product. It is therefore distressing to see how few girls take the trouble to acquire real skills. Why should this be so? Why are so few of the more interesting jobs and so many of the unskilled jobs held by women? The main reason is that girls lack the ambition to acquire skills and regard it as a waste of time. Only the exceptional girl sees a job or professional career as her life's work. Most are conditioned to seeing themselves living vicariously through their husband's careers, and are often prepared to sacrifice their own career projects completely in order to trail behind a husband who is chasing a will-o'-the-wisp success. Women's organisations, the trade unions and economists are increasingly concerned at the low level of vocational training and guidance for women in Britain. According to the Ministry of Labour only 6 per cent of the girls who took up employment in 1965 were apprenticed to skilled crafts. A further 2 per cent began training for professional qualifications, and 12 per cent undertook planned training below apprenticeship level. The number of girls at Government vocational training centres is negligible.

Statistics endorse the claim that it is harder for a girl than for a boy to obtain permission to be released from work during the day to attend vocational training. According to a committee set up by the Ministry of Education to study this problem, 30 per cent of all insured young male workers, compared with only 7 per cent of girls, were allowed day release in 1963. This situation should improve fairly quickly, however, once the new Industrial Training Boards really get under way, providing the training facilities can be set up and staffed.

FOUR

Married Women Working

'Women,' Vera Brittain once pointed out, 'have not yet achieved equal opportunities with men, but the woman who stays single can overcome by energy and determination most of the obstacles that remain. It is the married woman who still flounders in the morass of inequality . . . the future of all women demands a dynamic solution of the married woman's problems. How shall she bear children and yet remain a self-sufficient human being?'[1]

It is a matter for argument as to whether women who go out to work or women who stay at home feel the problem more acutely. Once children are at school, the woman without some kind of job outside the home is likely to be bored, whereas the woman with a job often suffers from tensions and frustrations of another kind, and from gross overwork as well. The situation has attracted unlimited attention from sociologists and psychologists during the past twenty years, and the wife-mother-worker dilemma remains good journalistic material.

In May 1965, for instance, the Countess of Dartmouth addressed the 5,000 delegates and their wives at the annual conference of the National Association of Round Tables, at Bognor. The members of Round Tables, one should remember, are all in their twenties and thirties, the age groups most directly affected by the problems caused by mothers taking outside employment. The Countess, whose views on a number of subjects seem to many people to be not among the

Notes to this chapter are on page 174

most enlightened or best informed in Britain, was on an exceptionally good wicket. By the time the reporters and sub-editors of that mirror of the average man, the *Western Daily Press*, had dealt with her address, readers received it in the following form, under the heading WORKING WIVES ARE SLAVES.[2]

'Women today have gilded fetters.

'But millions are chained to the treadmill of job-home-husband-children, until they drop with exhaustion.

'There is no time for tenderness, no time for love, no time to comfort, inspire and guide.

'Women have lost their mystery and their glamour.

'They have therefore killed romance. Instead we have sex in its most revolting forms.

'Filthy books, filthy plays, filthy magazines are currently glorified, and there are the same kind of perversions and homosexuality that marked the decline and fall of the Roman Empire.'

Lady Dartmouth drew this picture of the wife who goes out to work:

'Women doing a man's job without his physical stamina, rushing off in the morning, rushing home at night clutching the food which they must cook for supper, rushing to clean the house, rushing to cope with the children—there is only time for a quick kiss and a quick "hello".

'Mothers today have no time to hear their children's problems or their prayers.

'Wives have no time to tell their husbands, "I love you"—but never mind, the instalments are almost paid on the new car.

'To help pay for such things as homes and cars 8,290,000 women went out to work. Everyone admired their achievements and success, but in the process what had gone wrong with British life?

'"Why is the divorce rate so shocking?" asked the Countess. "Why are the juvenile crime rates soaring? Why are the churches empty? Why are the illegitimacy rates so appalling?" They should say to themselves such things as:

'THAT they were never too tired to listen to their husbands' worries.

'THAT it was up to them to make a home a happy place for husband and children, to set high standards of kindness, decency and good manners and never forget to tell their husbands how much they loved them.'

This is traditional tub-thumping stuff, strongly reminiscent of Samuel Smiles eighty years earlier: 'Whenever women have been drawn from the home and family to enter upon other work, the result has been socially disastrous.'[3] The generalisations of Smiles and Lady Dartmouth may be absurd but are still extremely popular in some circles. For some women, unable to organise their lives to meet a double demand, results both for themselves and for their families have undoubtedly been disastrous, but for others the consequences of staying at home have been equally bad. A husband often has to choose between the alternative of a wife who devotes her whole time to ministering to his creature comforts and who finds these whole-time ministrations more unbearably tedious each year, and a wife whose personal life becomes enriched through having a job, but who finishes each day desperately weary, and haunted with feelings of guilt that perhaps her family have somehow suffered from being deprived of her attention.

The working-wife syndrome is certainly a reality, but it is futile to assume that it represents the norm. Writing to the *Lancet* in February 1966, Dr J. F. Hanratty said that, in his opinion, most working wives enjoy going out to work. 'Those who have a labour-saving home, an understanding and co-operative husband and a congenial job experience few difficulties.' An increasing minority, however, showed symptoms of nervous tension. 'Such signs are particularly common among those living on private housing estates. I always ask the patient to describe her average day in detail before I examine her. The usual story is: get up at 7 am or earlier; do some rapid housework, including breakfast for the family; leave home at 8 am; work all day—often standing all the time—shopping in the lunch break or on the way home; and return home to a bleak house with unmade beds, breakfast dishes unwashed, at about 6 pm. The evening is spent in catching up on neglected housework and the weekend in washing, shopping, cleaning and mending.'

Full examination would reveal no organic complaint, though the patient has 'often' convinced herself before seeing her doctor that she has some grave disease. The one constant finding is 'a coarse tremor of the outstretched hands'. The cause of this syndrome, says Dr Hanratty, is 'sheer overwork'.

It is, however, a syndrome displayed by only a minority of working women. In this, as in most other matters, it is the disorganised person who comes off worst, but it is blind and insulting to suggest that most women are disorganised. What is certainly true is that 'if the wife was to make a success of going out to work she needed the intelligence to plan a routine and the character to stick to it.'[4]

The working wife is well aware that she has long been a controversial figure. To some people even today she is a symbol of freedom, and to others a symbol of irresponsibility. This uncertainty as to her role and image may in itself be a source of strain, although less so, in all probability, now that it is normal to work. In Britain today more than half the women in the labour force are married, whereas in 1900 the proportion was about 20 per cent. There is no mystery as to the reason for such an increase. Most families nowadays have all their children within the first ten years of marriage. The great majority of women have finished with childbearing by the time they are thirty. In 1900 the age would have been nearer to forty-five. The expectation of life has gone up dramatically, especially for women, so that a woman of forty can now reasonably expect to live another thirty-seven years. If one adds to these changes the advances made in what might be called household technology, so that housework can now be accomplished better in a much shorter time, it is hardly surprising that wives want to take outside employment—and to hold it. An advertisement in *New Society* is shrewdly worded: 'Security of Employment for Women in Industry,' it runs, 'requires reliable methods of birth control.'[5]

As Pearl Jephcott has noted, the whole matter of married women working produces strong feelings.[6] 'None of these criticisms allow that wives might successfully divide their time between work and home. At least, none seem to grant the working-class wife this ability, for the stereotype condemning the wife who works invariably concentrates on her. Perhaps these wives would be less often accused of forsaking their homes if they could represent themselves as a "movement", or if they could find an advocate for their "rights" as forceful as Mrs Judith Hubbard in her plea for the employment of graduate wives.[7] Possibly the stereotypes derive in part from middle-class apprehensions at the increasing affluence of the working-class; or even from nostalgic memories of the army of resident domestics long since decimated by social and economic change.'

It is indeed significant that a good deal of the more vocal opposition to working-class women earning money in industry comes from middle and upper-middle-class women over the age of 45 who appear to resent the independence of their former source of domestic servants. This feeling is rationalised until it appears in the more respectable form to which Lady Dartmouth gave expression at Bognor. It is a class reaction, not a manifestation of anti-feminism, although many men are sympathetic towards it. Most of the Bermondsey women studied by the authors of *Married Women Working* (1962) appeared to take their factory work in their stride. In their interviews with the research team they gave the impression of being energetic and resourceful individuals, living the busiest of lives, much helped in their domestic affairs by co-operative husbands, and by sensibly brought up children. They appeared to devote their extra income largely to their well-kept and efficient-looking homes, to more ample meals, better clothes and shoes, and a holiday away. In all this they kept the children's welfare very closely in mind. Going out to work was trying physically, of course, but it was worth it. There was little evidence of feelings of guilt, and the practical difficulties were not insuperable. Often these women seemed to have laid hold on a new lease of life through their work.[8]

They were not feminists, they accepted domesticity as a normal part of their lives, and their children were well looked after. They were part of a community with a long tradition of working mothers and of techniques for dealing with the family organisation demanded by this dual role. So many Bermondsey children had a mother who worked that there was no reason for the individual child to feel odd or deprived.

A later, but very similar investigation, carried out among women in factories in South London and Lancashire, and among men in the same areas, was reported by Sheila Black in 1964.[9] Many of them were outspokenly anxious to continue working for as long as possible after their children left school, so that their lives should not be entirely home-bound and empty. Most of them worked the very popular evening shift. 'Their reasons for working were rarely financial. Or, if they were, few mentioned money and, when they did, they put it below such things as "I feel more in the swim when I'm at work".' The social aspects of employment were the most sought-after and valued, and the loneliness of home was repeatedly stressed. The feeling of being useful, of being somebody in the world, was important, as was the desire to keep one's mind actively alive and up-to-date. A good many of the women spoke of 'tyrannical' or 'dictator' or 'only-cares-about-Number-One' husbands. One said she had started work just to earn enough money to buy the newspapers and magazines *she* wanted to read instead of the one daily paper her husband took to work as soon as it was delivered. 'It's all very well for him,' she said. 'He's a lot older than me and left school at fourteen, besides not learning much when he was there.' Though education was rarely mentioned as such there was a strong suggestion that, as education improves, so more women will want employment in order to avoid becoming cabbages. Clues to this came mainly in the form of 'I don't like knowing less about the world and things like that than my son/daughter/younger sister/the teachers at my children's school meetings/neighbour.'

Few couples minded spending five evenings a week apart.[10] In fact, they were surprised that such a question should be put to them. Their reasoning was simple and practical. After a hard day at work a man 'wants to relax, take off his coat, put up his feet, and eat, smoke, drink, sleep or watch television'. After a hard day at home, a woman 'needs to get out of the house or go mad'. 'If she doesn't,' one of the husbands said, 'she expects me to chat her up and notice her, when I want to put that sort of thing off till I'm more relaxed.'

By 10.30, the husbands are in a better frame of mind to pay attention to their wives, and the wives, after such a short shift, have enough energy left to greet them and to entertain them with the sayings, doings progress and gossip of the factory. By that time, 'he's ready to switch off the television, because most of the fun's over and it often gets a bit serious.' Bedtime in these households was normally around 11.30, sometimes later. In most of the homes there was amicable agreement that an hour or an hour-and-a-half together was probably about the right length of time for midweek conversation, before all the possible topics ran out and boredom set in.

The men were happy and did not resent the extra money, but they made it clear that they would always like to be the main breadwinner in the household. They seemed to find the wife more interesting 'when she's not stuck at home' and said so. Nearly all of them commented on the extra effort their wives took in 'keeping their looks and clothes sense when they're going off to work among a lot of other critical cats.'

This seems a form of married life much to be preferred to what Simone de Beauvoir has described as 'a thousand evenings of vague small talk, blank silences, yawning over the newspaper, retiring at bedtime.' 'Married life assumes different forms in different cases. But for a great many women the day passes in much the same fashion. The husband leaves in the morning and the wife is glad to hear the door close behind him. She is free; the children go to school; she is alone; she attends to a thousand small tasks; her hands are busy but her mind is empty; what plans she has are for the family; she lives only for them; it relieves her ennui when they return. Her husband used to bring her flowers, a little present; but how foolish this would seem now. He is in no hurry to get home, dreading the all too frequent scene in which she takes a small revenge for her boredom and expresses her anticipated disappointment in an appearance hardly worth waiting for, and the husband is disappointed too even if she keeps silence on her wrongs. He is tired from his work and has a contradictory desire for rest and stimulation, which she fails to satisfy. The evening is dull: reading, radio, desultory talks; each remains alone under cover of this intimacy. The wife wonders with hope or apprehension whether tonight—at last—"something will happen". She goes to sleep disappointed, vexed, solaced as the case may be: and it is with pleasure that she will hear him slam the door next morning. Woman's lot is harder to bear in poverty and toil; it is lighter with leisure and diversion; but its design for living—ennui, waiting, disappointment—recurs in innumerable cases.'[11]

In Simone de Beauvoir's ideal state, each member of the pair remains independent and continues to grow as a person. 'The couple should not be regarded as a unit, a closed cell; rather each individual should be integrated as such in society at large, where each, whether male or female, can flourish with aid: then attachments can be formed in pure generosity with another individual equally adapted to the group attachments; they would be founded upon the acknowledgment that both are free.'[12]

Her idea of the feminine hell resembles that described by Betty Friedan from an American point of view in *The Feminine Mystique*. Modern America, she says, has turned 'Occupation housewife' into a mystique, and pressurised women to accept it as the most desirable, the most feminine, the most advanced of all destinies. Love, motherhood and the family had to absorb all a woman's creative energies.

'In the 1950s, sociologists and home economists reported puzzlement, and baffling inconsistencies, as to the amount of time American women were still spending on housework. Study after study revealed that American housewives were spending almost as many, or even more, hours a day on housekeeping as women thirty years earlier, despite the smaller, easier-to-care-for homes, and despite the fact that they had seven times as much capital equipment in housekeeping appliances. There were, however, some exceptions. Women who worked many hours a week outside the home—either in paid jobs or community work—did the housekeeping, on which the full-time housewife still spent sixty hours a week, in half the time. They still seemed to do all the home-making activities of the housewife—meals, shopping, cleaning, the children—but even with a thirty-five-hour work week on the job, their work week was only an hour and a half a day longer than the housewife's.

'That this strange phenomenon caused so little comment was due to the relative scarcity of such working women. For the even stranger phenomenon, the real significance of which the mystique hid, was the fact that, despite the growth of the American population and the movement of that population from farm to city with the parallel growth of American industry and professions, in the first fifty years of the twentieth century the proportion of American women working outside the home increased very little indeed, while the proportion of American women in the professions actually declined. From nearly half the nation's professional force in 1930, women had dropped to only 35 per cent in 1960, despite the fact that the number of women college graduates had nearly tripled. The phenomenon was the great increase in the numbers of educated women choosing to be just housewives.'[13]

The result is a profound, widespread, nagging dissatisfaction. A ridiculously large number of American women are not using their abilities. With their children grown up they lead pseudo-lives with no real purpose in them. They are victims of a problem without a name, 'which is simply the fact that

American women are kept from growing to their full human capacity', and which is 'taking a far greater toll of the physical and mental health of our country than any known disease.'

It marks a major educational failure, for which there is only one cure. 'Educators at every women's college, at every university, junior college, and community college, must see to it that women make a lifetime commitment (call it a "life plan", a "vocation", a "life purpose" if that dirty word *career* has too many celbate connotations) to a field of thought, to work of serious importance to society. They must expect the girl as well as the boy to take some field seriously enough to want to pursue it for life.' For some years, while their children are growing up, they will be able to work only sporadically or part-time.

It could well be, however, that, after winning the battle to find suitable part-time work for themselves and often overcoming their husbands' opposition to their taking it, many British women are finding the prize snatched from them. The Selective Employment Tax, coming on top of the existing insurance regulations, makes part-time work expensive and troublesome to organise, so that most firms try to reduce or abolish it. To judge by what has happened already, this is likely to hit part-time workers in the service industries, especially retailing, particularly hard.[14] Although not intended as such, SET may turn out to be the most anti-feminist measure of modern times.

Women forced out of the labour market for any cause may of course vote against the political party they hold responsible. More immediately, their men may demand a substantial rise in wages to compensate for the loss of the second income. At the moment a large proportion of families are only able to maintain their standard of living against the pressure of steadily rising costs by means of the extra money the wives earn. As long as cars and holidays away from home are felt to be essential features of family wellbeing, opposition to women working is a philosophical luxury in which few men indulge with much conviction, although they may continue to pay lip service to the idea that woman's place is in the home.

The most important factor in the situation, both socially and politically, is that such a large number of married women are determined to take outside employment of some kind. For nearly thirty years the economy has been more or less able to meet their wishes, with the result that Britain now ranks third in Europe, equal with Austria, in the proportion of women in the total labour force. Only in the Soviet Union and Finland is the figure higher.

No one would wish to force women on to the labour market if they neither need nor want to work, but the fact remains that many women find housekeeping and children neither a full-time nor a satisfying job. It has been estimated that, if present trends continue—which of course they may not—British industry will be short of 200,000 workers by 1970. The situation may be made more difficult when the school-leaving age is eventually raised to sixteen. The only major pool of labour left is composed of women, especially the older married women. Guilt and social pressure keep many at home, although there are great regional differences in this, and there is a vital need for labour and management to be educated to provide conditions of employment which the women themselves feel to be reasonable. These would certainly include the provision of more part-time work and more nursery facilities. A real attempt to provide day-nurseries on an adequate scale would go a long way towards reducing the high rates of absenteeism and labour turnover which cause employers to be prejudiced against married women as employees. Yet as a report of the National Labour Women's Advisory Committee makes clear, far from expanding to meet demand, local authorities have restricted nurseries to what they call priority cases. During the war there were more than 1,500 day nurseries with 70,000 places. In 1967 there were only 455 day nurseries with 21,000 places, with some areas not catered for at all.

Some observers believe that a return to full-time domesticity may have already begun. The *Economist* has commented[15] that 'in so far as this return to female domesticity might be a new trend in a more affluent society, it would be right to accept it as an indication of the way in which the British people (probably sensibly) now prefer to live.' This reference to 'a more affluent society' would seem to imply that, for manual workers, men's earnings are becoming sufficient to maintain the family standard of living at a satisfying level. This seems doubtful. Most families want to buy and run a car, the prized badge of a member of the affluent society, and, even with the help of a wife's earnings, most motorists in Britain are only just able to meet the hire-purchase payments and maintain the vehicle in a tolerable condition, while meeting the other demands of the affluent society. When the Government enforces something better than the present miserably low standard of car maintenance, keeping the car on the road will be even more expensive. The man who is unable to afford a car is not likely to derive much comfort from the fact that his wife has all day at home to clean and polish it. And, quite apart from the financial aspects, if women have shown themselves so anxious to work to keep themselves mentally alive, why should this elusive thing, 'a more affluent society', persuade the ordinary run of women to abandon their precious and hard-won links with the outside world?

The convoluted argument has been advanced that if modern homes are so easy to run that house-bound women become bored and frustrated, then the answer is to create additional, new-style housework that fills every nook and cranny of the day. The case for this has been put by Professor Dennis Gabor,[16] in an address to a conference of scientists, industrialists, bankers and investors, most of whom, one might think, had incomes large enough to make a working wife economically unnecessary. Professor Gabor said there was a good and bad way of running a home. 'The bad way is to make crockery and cutlery expendable, to simplify shopping to card-punching, use freeze-dried food, reduce cooking to the pushing of buttons, and leave cleaning to the electronic housemaid.

The good way is gracious living, with property instead of consumption, and with pride in property which makes housework rewarding instead of boring.'

So does the property-minded housewife spend hours polishing the antiques, reading books about them and attending sales to buy more? Does she have experts in to consult about cleaning the household Rembrandts or re-upholstering the Sheraton chairs? Or does most of her time go in thinking out dinner parties to grace her elegantly furnished rooms? If this is what Professor Gabor means—and no other explanation offers itself—we are back to the Victorian recipe for middle-class living, and any attempt at its revival seems ludicrously far-fetched. He seems in any case to be oddly out of touch with what is actually happening. Instead of conjuring up more and more gracious things for our property-proud women to fill their time with, 'we are now,' he says, 'going the opposite way, in the direction of women having less to do and yet being bored to death with their housework. We shall have to reverse this tendency if our civilisation is not to come to grief by the bad nerves of its dissatisfied women.'

Simone de Beauvoir's description of housework has not been surpassed. 'Few tasks are more like torture of Sisyphus than housework with its endless repetition; the clean becomes soiled, the soiled is made clean, over and over, day after day. The housewife wears herself out making time. She makes nothing, simply perpetuates the present. She never senses conquest of a positive Good, but rather indefinite struggle against negative Evil . . . Washing, ironing, sweeping, ferreting out fluff from under wardrobes—all this halting of decay is also the denial of life; for time simultaneously creates and destroys and only its negative aspect concerns the housekeeper.'[17]

What does not seem to have occurred to Professor Gabor is the possibility of women dividing their time between their homes and an outside job. The last thing any sensible society wants is to have to live with the bad nerves of its dissatisfied women, or for that matter of its dissatisfied men, but much of that dissatisfaction comes from the knowledge that one has talents and skills and training for which society appears to have no use. The point that has escaped Professor Gabor is that it is no more than justice and common sense to allow people to do what they want to do. If a woman is genuinely happiest at home, then home is the place for her to be. If she can only fulfil herself by having a job as well as a family, who is Professor Gabor or anyone else to be inventing mod-housework in order to keep her under her own roof?

As Dr Kellmer Pringle, Director of the National Bureau for Co-operation in Child Care, has said, 'It is quite dreadful that a woman should feel she should have to apologise for being a full-time housewife and mother.'[18] Dr Pringle referred to what he described as 'the terrific drives to get married women back to work'. Such campaigns, he admitted, might be necessary, but he thought it a mistake for mothers to feel they should think in terms of outside occupations as soon as possible. He believed there was 'a need to reorientate our values so that a woman does not need to apologise for looking after her home and children.'

It is equally unreasonable to expect a married woman to apologise because she works, although many well-qualified women experience great difficulties when trying to find suitable work after having been out of employment for a few years. A very typical case was that of a qualified occupational therapist with two young children, living in South London. She wanted to return to work, having made proper arrangements for her children to be looked after during the day, but found, although occupational therapists are scarce, that no local authority would consider her. 'On enquiring the reason for this (which annoyed most of them),' she wrote to *The Times*, 'I was told it was because of my marital situation, which they considered "unreliable". One authority said that they would reconsider my application with pleasure if I was prepared to say that the post came first and not the children.'[19]

The demand was brutal, but not altogether absurd, since all authorities have had bitter experience of married women trying to carry out full-time professional work—far more demanding than factory work—without reliable and regular domestic help. This information does not come from employers alone. Dr Viola Klein organised a system of diary-keeping by members of the British Federation of University Women, to show in detail how they combined working with running a home. 'All but six of the women taking part in the survey,' she reported,[20] 'have paid domestic help of one kind or another, whether a charwoman, an au-pair girl, or a resident housekeeper. It is evident from the diaries that the relative ease with which a woman manages her "two roles" is in direct proportion to the amount and quality of domestic help she gets. Only one woman in the sample has "had enough" and is about to give up: she is a school teacher with three children under five and no domestic help. To have a reliable person who relieves her of part of her household routine is evidently crucial for a woman with a family who wishes to carry on a profession.'

A great deal of information, some of it surprising, about graduate women in employment is to be found in the book sponsored by the British Federation of University Women, *Graduate Women at Work*, published in 1965. This reveals that most of such women do in fact work, strongly contradicting the common belief that women 'waste' their expensive education by retiring to marriage and a wholly domesticated life at an early age. Nearly 75 per cent were in paid employment, almost 60 per cent of them full-time. In the age groups twenty-five to thirty-four, forty-five to fifty-four and fifty-five to sixty-four, 79 per cent had a paid job, a percentage that few people would have guessed. Even among the thirty-five to forty-four-year-olds the figure was 69 per cent. As might have been expected, the more highly qualified a woman is, the more likely she is to have a job. Sixty-five per cent of those with only a first degree worked, but for those with high degrees or professional qualifications the figure was 77 per cent and 83 per cent of these women worked full-time.

Most of these graduates were employed in some form of education. Fifty-five per cent were in schools and the remainder in universities, technical colleges and colleges of education. Medicine and dentistry accounted for 25 per cent, but social work only 4 per cent. The numbers holding executive positions in industry were too small to distinguish as a separate category.

Only 19 per cent were prepared to admit that money was the greatest incentive to work. The higher the husband's salary the lower was the proportion of wives in a paid job, though even where the husband was earning over £3,000, 50 per cent of them had a paid job. For the others it was the interest of the work which had persuaded them to return, or a combination of several factors, including guilt at not using their training. (The burden of guilt seemed inevitable, since they also felt guilty about leaving children.)

Mrs Jessie Barnard's study of American academic women, published in 1965, showed that in America women with academic interests appeared to be turning their backs on academic life.[21]

The proportion of women on college and university teaching staffs had dropped about 10 per cent since the 1930s. This was not because of any discrimination; the root cause was almost certainly that academic life, with its constant tensions and struggles to keep up to date, had become less attractive than a number of alternative careers, government service, for instance, or law or journalism.

A doctor's degree is an essential piece of personal equipment for an academic career in America and the long period of hard work needed in order to obtain it is something that few women are able to face. They may begin their research, but if they marry and have children they will almost certainly have to give it up. They are likely to marry fellow academics, also working for a higher degree, and they may feel that their main responsibility is to make life as easy as possible for their husbands, who need the PhD more than they do themselves; significantly only 10 per cent of American PhDs are women. If they do somehow preserve the stamina and the willpower to complete their doctoral thesis, they will in most cases move to a university which provides an acceptable post for the husband, but not necessarily or probably for the wife. One of the saddest features of the American situation is the number of talented women who give up working for a doctorate and reconcile themselves to the humble university jobs—laboratory supervision, introductory courses and tutorials—while their husbands progress to professorships and continue with their own independent research.

Mrs Barnard shows fairly convincingly that, in America at least, universities are not the most satisfying places for women to work in. Unmarried women, including professors, are afraid of beginning any sort of public exchange of views with their colleagues, for fear of being considered sexually aggressive, and married women are similarly reticent, in case they should happen to do better than their husbands. One of Mrs Barnard's informants, a scientist, analysed his wife's abilities in this way. 'She was tentatively and temperamentally academic when we were married, just enough to help earn my way through graduate school. Then she did what marriage meant to both of us—settled back into the roles of wife, mother, hostess and housekeeper.'

The situation is probably not very different on the British side of the Atlantic. A special survey of the subsequent history of 105 women doctors who graduated at Sheffield between 1930 and 1952 discovered that 80 per cent were married—over half of them to doctors—and that nearly 90 per cent were still living in the United Kingdom. All but one of the single women and about two-thirds of the married women were working. Those who graduated after 1947 married sooner, had larger families and did less full-time work than those who qualified before that year. Some of the more recent graduates married during their training and had children before finishing the preregistration year of hospital work. If they intend to return to medical work later, they may find it difficult to do so.

Those married to doctors tended to have larger families than those who had non-medical husbands and yet were able to do more full-time medical work. This can only be because they were in the exceptionally favourable situation of being able to work with their husbands, and therefore in a sense at home.

The proportion of married women doctors working is by some people felt to be much too small, however. In an angry letter to *The Times*, Sir George McRobert described the utilisation of married women in Britain as 'miserable', and went on: 'I should like to say that of the many hundreds of Asian medical women who have been my pupils during the past five decades I have never heard of one who has given up her professional work for more than a few brief weeks. Some have worked unto death and others until old age has enforced retirement. This, of course, is largely due to the joint family system whereby one finds three or four generations living together. It has its disadvantages, but in this country we suffer from isolation of the generations.

'I have just received a letter from a London suburb from a young Asian woman doctor announcing the birth of her first child and that "my mother-in-law has just flown into London to take the baby back home so that my post-graduate studies will not be interrupted". The education of medical women was one of the best things we did in Asia. If only we could ensure an equally good return for the energy and money put into the education of medical women in this country.'[22]

One not unimportant reason why many married women are discouraged from working is the taxation system. This is particularly oppressive for professional women, such as doctors, who earn well and are mostly married to men in the same fortunate position. 'Marriage,' wrote Sheila Black in the *Financial Times*, 'is expensive for the big income earners.'[23] In Britain, where the husband's and wife's joint income does not exceed £5,000 a year, there are tax advantages in being married; above that figure the situation changes. In the United States, taxation is more progressive over the whole income scale, and although people with low earnings are rather more severely taxed, those with larger individual and family incomes are usually more favourably placed.

There is a strong case for allowing each couple to choose between joint or separate tax assessments on their respective incomes, which would also obviate another anomaly resented by a substantial number of women—having to disclose their incomes to their husbands. A wife may ask for a separate assessment of her earnings, but her income is still regarded as secondary and joined to her husband's and is consequently revealed to him, while his may always remain a secret from her. All that a separate assessment achieves is a fairer sharing out of the tax burden. The outdated British taxation laws are still based on the theory that married women cease to be individuals once they become wives. Their rights in joint property have been radically changed during the past century, but they are still classed with children and idiots under most of the laws relating to finance. Perhaps one of the most galling things for a wife about being a second-class citizen is the method of repayment of any tax overpaid in previous years: even if the overpayment was extracted on her income, her husband gets the reimbursement. Small matters of this kind do undoubtedly take some of the zest and satisfaction out of earning.

Even among the well-informed there is much disagreement about tax relief for women at work.[24] The most frequently heard criticism is that suggested tax reliefs such as on paid domestic help would be unfair to low-income groups, who pay little or no tax anyway, and who employ no domestic help, and that they would not allow the community to discriminate between the jobs it might want to subsidise in this way—medicine or social work—and other jobs that it might be glad to tax.

Apart from taxation, one of the main discouragements married women have to face when thinking of returning to work is the realisation that their knowledge and skills are out of date. Attempts to stimulate realistically planned refresher courses have mostly been half-hearted and badly geared to the domestic pattern of the women they are meant to be helping. An imaginative effort has been made by the architects: in 1964, the Architectural Association completed a pilot course for bringing qualified women architects into touch with new technical developments.[25] One of the indispensable functions of this course is to give the women more confidence, as they bring their knowledge up to date. The first part of it deals with, among other things, new materials, new methods and new social demands. Equally important from the students' point of view is the confidence the course gives to their prospective employers. Hitherto the older woman returning to an architect's office finds herself stuck with mere draughtsman's work because it is felt that she is too far out of touch to be given anything more responsible.

The idea that work can only be done on an employer's premises may have become too rigid. Probably far more women than at present could carry out various forms of professional work perfectly satisfactorily in their own homes. The Association for the Employment of Mothers was founded for this purpose in 1963, and has provided mothers with do-it-at-home work in photography, translating, dressmaking, psychiatry, indexing, cooking, computing. The Association is well thought of by employers because it has insisted from the beginning on absolute professionalism in quality and deadlines.

A specialised self-help organisation working along somewhat similar lines is Freelance Programmers Limited, run by Mrs Steve Shirley, to begin with from her home in Buckinghamshire. A newspaper advertisement set it going:

> 1 IBM and 1 Leo programmers wanted for full-time assignments based at home, mobile London. Wonderful chance, *but hopeless for anti-feminists*. Also many opportunities for retired programmers (female) to work part-time at home, London and Midlands. Telephone and impeccable references essential.[26]

Mrs Shirley, formerly a programmer with a big computer company, gathered together twenty out-of-circulation programmers like herself who 'because of their children could not consider going back to a job that wanted them on an all-or-nothing basis.'[27] After six months' experience she had come to two conclusions, that a centrally located office, with one or two full-time staff, was essential, and that the organisation needed a few more mobile women, able to travel around the country when occasion demanded. These improvements have made it possible to make better and more extensive use of the services of the house-bound, and in its present form Freelance Programmers may well be a model for similar groups of professionally trained women. Another field of activity which has already developed along similar lines is part-time work on scientific indexing, abstracting and sub-editing, where it is easier to maintain a high standard of accuracy when working shorter hours.

Yet the Women's Information & Study Centre[28] and the Women's Employment Federation, which receive a great many enquiries each year about employment opportunities, both say that most of the women who write to them want to get out of their homes, not to find work they can do at home. 'In spite of the convenient male illusion about how fulfilling it is to think about socks and potatoes, the jobs for which their years of domesticity might seem to have fitted them are often just exactly what they do not want.'[29]

FIVE

The Mark 2 Wife

The Mark 2 Wife,[1] briefly defined, appears to be an increasingly popular alternative to the more traditional arrangement of Mark 1 wife plus up-front mistress. She is the replacement helpmate acquired by the ambitious man in industry, commerce or politics at a stage in his career when he has come to feel, sensibly or stupidly, that the Mark 1 version, which has given him adequate, possibly even excellent service for the past fifteen or twenty years, no longer matches up to the social and inspirational tasks required of her. Personal observation and discussions with well-informed people suggest that the Mark 2 Wife is a quite commonly found feature of the British business and professional scene, but it is still rather against the code of polite and influential society to discuss the phenomenon, and perhaps the inevitability, of her existence.

There appear to be three main reasons for the Mark 2 Wife—early first marriage, ruthless commercial competition, and a refusal on the part of both employers and society to face up to the expensive fact that wives have a professional half-life which somehow must be renewed if they are to be happy as human beings and effective as the accomplices of influential men. Some wives, blessed with exceptional energy and intelligence, manage to organise this necessary process of personal renewal without outside help and from their own resources. For these fortunate few the miserable fate of becoming superannuated and junked does not arise. Over a period of years

Notes to this chapter are on page 176

they pass continuously and imperceptibly from Mark 1 to Mark 2. But many more fail to keep pace with their husband's moves up the ladder. One of three possible futures awaits them. They may have to watch themselves becoming progressively more abandoned to an almost wholly domestic existence, playing little or no part in the social and public life surrounding their husband's career. They may, provided they are physically sufficiently presentable, be admitted as more or less non-talking accessories at those cocktail-parties, dinners and receptions which are conventionally two-sex affairs. Or they may decide to cultivate their own garden and build up a distinct career or group of interests for themselves, unconnected with their husband's work and ambitions. None of these courses will necessarily lead to a total fading-away of the marriage, but where the possession of a contemporary model company-wife is considered, rightly or wrongly, to be an important part of a man's business success, the wife who is unmistakably yesterday's model, or no model at all, has small hope of survival in any positive or creative sense. The best she can expect is to be shunted, baffled and embittered, on to a siding or a branch line.

Sometimes this is only to her credit. She may find the aims and methods of her husband's work so repulsive or degrading that she would prefer to remain entirely detached from them. We are not all born to believe that, in order to become Prime Minister or the world's biggest canner of beans or dealer in real estate or manufacturer of army uniforms, the ends justify the means. The most intelligent and most beautiful and most socially gifted of wives has a perfect right to loathe and despise salesmen's conventions, political rallies, sycophantic dinner-parties and masonic ladies' nights, and the attitude to life of which they form part.

Sometimes, but not very often, the lid is taken off this particular social kettle in public. One such occasion was in March 1965, when the BBC, greatly daring, put out a television programme which discussed some of the pros and cons of freemasonry, and which included a representation of a masonic initiation ceremony. It was followed by, in addition to a flood of mail and telephone calls to the BBC itself, a considerable newspaper correspondence. One of the published letters came from a woman, who, not surprisingly, preferred to sign herself merely 'Freemason's Wife'. It needs no comment.

'My husband became a Mason, to my great distress, several years after we were married; it has ever since been a source of differences between us. The enforced secrecy alienates husband and wife, and throws up artificial barriers between them, which I do not feel the annual "Ladies' Evening" counteracts.

'The BBC programme was not a good one, but I was grateful to it for vindicating what had before been only an inherent distaste for the craft. The ceremonies enacted may have contained inaccuracies but in substance I am sure they were correct. I was sickened by the loss of personal dignity suffered by the candidate and the blood-curdling promises exacted under oath. To know that my husband takes part in such antics lessens my respect for him (I was heartened to hear one Mason on the programme comment: "I wondered what my wife would think").

'It would be interesting to know how many wives have felt a loss of closeness with their husbands as a result of masonic practice. I should be delighted to discover I was not alone in my reaction.'[2]

This 'loss of personal dignity', which so shocked the Mason's wife is not, of course, peculiar to Masonic ceremonies. To a greater or lesser degree it can be found in the ritual of half a dozen oath-bound male societies in Britain, and it is a feature of the barbarous initiation ceremonies which accompany the arrival of a new recruit at certain factories. Women, for the most part, are not well-informed about these things. When they do hear about them in any detail, their reaction is likely to include disgust, and disbelief that adults can indulge in such childish obscenities. It is almost impossible to imagine women taking part in, for instance, the redbrick-university ceremonies described by the sociologist, Maurice Punch, in his famous *New Society* article 'The Student Ritual'. 'An American student broke down and cried, because, it was later learnt, a close friend had died during an exacting initiation ceremony in a college fraternity in the United States, and he was apprehensive as to what awaited him!' After tribal savagery of this kind, a Masonic initiation is almost gentle and civilised, with nothing worse than infantilism and loss of personal dignity involved.

Freemasonry is not, in fact, the wholly male activity which most people imagine it to be. An organisation known as International Co-Freemasonry, or Mixed Masonry, has wide support.[3] It was founded in France in 1893 by Mlle Maria Desraines, a strong advocate of women's rights, and the first British lodge was set up in 1907. Co-Freemasonry has had close association with Theosophy. Annie Besant herself was a strong supporter. The headquarters are still in Paris, and the Supreme Council consists mainly of women.

In Britain, there is a Craft Freemasonry organisation for women only. The Order of Women Freemasons was founded in 1908 and in 1965 had 5,500 members. One of them, living in Bristol, told James Dewar that her husband was a prominent Freemason and that, although the rituals used by the women's lodges were the same as practised by the men, she and her husband retired to different rooms to learn the ceremonies.[4] A photograph published in Mr Dewar's book shows the installation of the Lady Grand Master of the Order in 1937. All the women present appear to be over the age of fifty. The Grand Masters (why is she not called the Grand Mistress?) are both wearing aprons of the usual Masonic type. The other women present are apronless with large white scarves across their shoulders, and carry handbags.

It is not easy to discover what male Freemasons feel about this feminisation of the Craft. The Grand Lodge of England makes clear that one of the basic principles of Lodge recognition is that membership shall be confined to men. As Mr Dewar puts it, in a not altogether happy phrase, 'There is to be no Masonic intercourse with mixed lodges or organisations that admit women members.'[5] 'British Freemasons I have spoken to,' he says, 'seem to enjoy the movement's exclusive masculinity, particularly clergyman members. Dr Baxter, Church of Scotland, remarked, "I thought it was a good thing for me to have an all-male society amongst all my other things. A minister is compelled to do a lot of duties that bring him in touch with women only." ' The comment of the minister at the City Temple, the Rev Leonard Griffiths, was 'I think this is a man's world and I think every man needs to get into that world occasionally and Masonry is perhaps one expression of this. Certainly in the churches I've always been depressed by the fact that there seemed to be a much larger proportion of women there than men. I like to be with men and perhaps that's one reason why I enjoy attending a meeting of a Masonic lodge.'[6]

The number of women Freemasons in Britain is small, bearing no comparison with the figure of one-in-twenty adult males now reckoned to be a Mason. Most women in families with Masonic links are firmly on the sidelines and excluded from the secrets.

If a wife sees her future as involving an endless succession of Ladies' Nights or other equally uncongenial public events, she may well feel that her self-respect demands parting company with the man responsible. In this respect as in others, incompatibility can become plain at forty although invisible at thirty. Some company-wives are also expected to give not only their tolerance, but their enthusiastic support to unscrupulous commercial practices, and some men's methods of making money unfortunately need a wife to match.

Our immediate concern, however, is with a different problem, that of the woman whose interests and experience stand still, while those of her husband are widening all the time; the woman whose mind and confidence have gone into what might appear to be an impossibly deep freeze during the years she has spent inside the domestic world of children and housework; the woman whose head is filled with yesterday's information and values and who talks yesterday's language; the woman who for one reason and another has failed to grow and develop in a way which allows her to adapt herself to the needs of a husband on the way up.

In the days when successful men tended to marry late, or at any rate later than they do now, the situation was different in several important respects. In general, they married women whose social abilities were required straight away, not in ten or fifteen years' time. They were much more likely, partly because of their own background and partly because they were already well up the ladder of success, to choose wives who were already reasonably familiar with the habits of influential people. Their wives may, it is true, have been expected to bear them more children than would be thought acceptable today, but as a compensation, from the moment they were married they were provided with domestic help on a scale which would now be considered either utopian or criminal. And, most important of all, they were marrying and establishing themselves in positions of power at a time before the concept of the Executive Wife had been invented. Their wives were married to them, not to the International Saltcellar Corporation.

We could describe this change in another way. In the first half of the twentieth century, top jobs in politics, industry and commerce were almost invariably held down by ex-public schoolboys from moneyed families. Their wives were not required to be domesticated, but were free to be true companions to their husbands. Today these top positions usually go to men with the right educational background, regardless of the social or economic standing of their fathers. Increasingly often nowadays they are ex-grammar schoolboys whose only source of income is what they earn. Their wives are therefore tied to their homes and children in a way that earlier generations of businessmen's wives were not. Today's husbands are working under ever-increasing pressure and at great speed, and can cease to be human beings. They often have difficulty in readjusting mentally to the necessarily slower tempo of family surroundings. This results in a lack of communication between husband and wife and a consequent rift in their relationship. It is easy for the Mark 2 Wife, rooted in the public and not the family world, to take over at this point.

Not, of course, that it is only recently that ambitious men have found their progress eased by ambitious wives, able and anxious to play an effective social role. History, particularly political history, is full of such ladies. What is new in the present situation is the extent to which first marriages appear to be regarded as biological, temporary and, from a career point of view, subsequently regrettable, and to which, with a more permissive attitude towards divorce, the Mark 2 Wife is felt to be not only inevitable but even desirable. Observation suggests that she will usually be considerably younger than the Man-on-the-way-to-the-top she is marrying—the human-interest advertisements of the shipping companies and airlines provide interesting confirmation of this—and in nearly all instances this second marriage will be childless, although the Mark 2 Wife may very well have children by a previous husband.

There is no reason to put the Mark 2 Wife on a pedestal. She may be more clued-up and more presentable in various ways than her predecessor, but sometimes on the contrary she is nothing more than a toy for the successful man who finds himself unable to accept the wifely criticism that comes from Mark 1. Because both she and her husband are at a later stage in their lives, she may tend to be more relaxed and have a more agreeable personality than the go-getting Mark 1, whose persistence was largely responsible for the success of her husband. But for many successful men with Mark 2 wives the Jewish saying 'The very altar sheds tears over the man who sends away the wife of his youth' is all too appropriate. They find that they have put themselves into a position where they can never relax again. It is useless for the tycoon to compain that he is tired after a couple of late nights, because Mark 2 will be bursting with energy and enthusiasm for the next cocktail party. If he shows signs of rebelling, he knows that his wife will be on the look-out for a Mark 3 Husband.

The strain of keeping up with his wife in private as well as his colleagues in public may prove too much for him and he may die, a modern martyr, of one of the stress diseases.

One recalls the case of an enormously successful conductor who was married first to another successful artist, a singer, and then subsequently married the family's au-pair girl, who had little education and no English. This is perhaps a little exceptional. More generally, one of the great strengths of the Mark 2 marriage is that both parties to it are fairly seasoned veterans and do not go into it with clouds of illusion.

There are, of course, Mark 2 Husbands as well as Mark 2 Wives, for quite a number of gifted, ambitious women have the misfortune to marry incompatibly stupid or boorish or unsuccessful men, who in due course are shed. The parting of two people of unequal intelligence and interests is one thing—such unions normally give rise to endless frustration and unhappiness—but the replacement of a wife whose main demerit is that she has been compelled to live in a personal world distinct from that of her husband is a different matter, and one which represents a serious failure on the part of society rather than of the individuals directly involved.

Ironically, the big world of industry, commerce and politics is all too likely to breed men with small and even childish interests and values, while the little world of the home and private activity can help some women's minds and personalities to expand and grow. When men have to earn their living in a mental straitjacket, as they often do, it is not difficult for a wife's interests to outstrip those of her husband. All too often the husband's energies and interests are confined almost entirely to work and to possibly one hobby, and he may well realise and resent this. Nor is it unknown, even in today's meritocratic world, for the Mark 1 Wife to outstrip her husband in social poise, particularly where the tycoon or successful politician has started from humble origins.

If the education of intelligent girls before they marry is so out of touch with modern conditions and modern needs that they find themselves without either the will or the inner resources to keep their minds alive during the concentrated domesticity of their twenties and early thirties, then our educational system does indeed need very drastic overhaul. If bright boys are in the habit of marrying dumb girls—for some reason this appears to be especially common among scientists and technologists—then urgent attention should be given to their education as well. The clever boy, the first member of his family to receive a higher education, who works so hard during his sixth-form and university period that he has neither time nor energy to get his social and emotional bearings, is all too likely to link himself up in his early twenties with a wife of limited interests and abilities who may be something of an embarrassment to him when he begins to be considered for more responsible posts in industry or the scientific Civil Service.

What are perhaps unfairly called 'Harwell marriages' are a sad feature of our age. One sometimes hears as an excuse the old complaint that there are not enough educated girls to go around, so that the poor PhDs are positively compelled to marry inferior products. Much the same explanation used to be given as to why dukes married chorus girls: there were not enough lively peers' daughters in the market. But the dukes were at least marrying for the present. The Harwell PhDs and the managing directors in-the-making are being asked to do something much more difficult, to marry for the unpredictable future at a time when they have every reason to be preoccupied with the present.

Assuming social mobility continues to its present extent, the first marriage of many of the most influential members of society may increasingly tend to be for procreation and the second as a contribution to power and success. Before becoming reconciled to this, however, it might be worth thinking harder and more imaginatively both about the deadening and narrowing effect of the executive life itself and about forms of mind-broadening, mind-preserving, appearance-preserving adult education that really meet the needs of young women with young children. The growing list of companies and political organisations which make a practice of vetting the wife before giving the husband a move upwards[7] could, perhaps, be persuaded that they, too, have some responsibility in helping wives to keep themselves up to date with the pulse and values of the great world. Industrial subsidies to help industrial wives to avoid becoming cabbages would seem to be no more than elementary social justice.[8] Firms more integrated into the life of the community and less little self-contained worlds of their own could probably help to discover suitable paid or unpaid part-time jobs for wives, in the district if not in their own organisation. Industry might also consider more carefully its potentiality as a marriage-wrecker through its ingrained habit of setting up its executives with secretaries young enough to be their daughters.

The main problem, however, may be more fundamental and hardly recognised as yet for the human revolution it involves. It is well shown in Antonioni's film *Le Desert Rouge*, a study of woman's place in an industrial society. The wife, the central figure, is educated, free, but with no real function; her husband runs a petroleum refinery, is extremely busy and often away. She, more than she would have been in any previous generation, is 'the warrior's rest'. The world controlled by technocrats is not her world, but the technocrat has all the satisfaction and fulfilment he needs. Apart from the legal advantages to his children, there is no reason for her to be married at all; she carries a hollow title. She is shut out, both practically and psychologically, from the world that makes all the things she uses every day. The master-level of industrial society is production; the kings of the modern world are the people who have a stake in it. Woman is condemned to be no more than the arch-consumer. The sexual division as presented by *Le Desert Rouge* is no longer man-woman, but producer-consumer.

A similar view of woman's modern predicament is offered by Oriana Fallaci in her well-named book *The Useless Sex*. There is, however, a fallacy in the argument. Women can avoid this situation of inferiority by becoming technocrats. If a substantial number of them do not do so, women as a whole seem inevitably condemned to become second-grade citizens.

SIX

Women and Public Life

The Gallup Poll studies of voting at every British general election since 1945 have established that there is no such thing as the women's vote. Class differences are much more important than sex differences. In general, working-class men and women both vote Labour and the middle-class of both sexes vote Conservative. Within both classes, there is some tendency for more women than men to favour the Conservatives: in a group of 100 men and 100 women there are likely to be about six more Conservatives among the women than among the men. One explanation for this is that women have on average a longer expectation of life than men—there are nearly 1,500,000 more women than men above the age of sixty-five—and in Britain old people have tended to favour the Conservative Party. In 1964, according to the Gallup Poll, elderly women preferred the Conservatives by a margin of about three to two. 'These women were denied the vote at twenty-one and reached maturity at a time when the Liberals, not Labour, were the second party in the land.'[1] (So far as political personalities are concerned, on the Gallup evidence, men certainly appear to be better informed than women. Sixty per cent of men are high scorers when asked to recall names of party leaders and Cabinet posts; the figure for women is only 36 per cent.)

The Conservative Central Council cherishes its women voters. 'Women' it is confident, 'vote Conservative because they are conservative. They are home-centred. They want

Notes to this chapter are on page 177

security for their families and are not prepared to risk what they have got.'[2]

Sociologists give different reasons. Their verdict is that many women are Conservative because they are cross-pressured. These women have conflicting allegiances between home and work and swing in an unpredictable and disconcerting fashion in their loyalties. The way they vote may well decide the election. They have emerged because of the long term changes in the occupational structure. Most of them are white-collar workers who married manual workers and have gone back to white-collar jobs. They are apt to vote Tory with the boss and the people at the office when things are going prosperously, but they vote Labour with their husbands if times are bad. They are both the despair and the delight of the political parties and to men with firmly established loyalties they are a proof of feminine flightiness and irresponsibility.

The shifts in population have tended to increase the Conservative vote in certain parts of the country. When women move from north to south they are quite likely to acquire Conservative habits, changing their vote with their house. Their vote can be significant if they happen to have moved from a northern Labour stronghold to a marginal seat in the Home Counties.

The public image of Conservative women *en masse* is not always appealing. Some of these ladies, including, as a careful look round the annual Party Conference is likely to reveal, a number of the more prominent, make it easier to justify the anti-feminist view that politics and women are better apart. The problem was examined in 1964 at a reception given at the Central Office by the Conservative Women's National Advisory Committee, where according to one report, 'several representatives of both sexes admitted ruefully, in response to some gentle prodding, that there is more than a grain of truth in the caricature version of Tory womanhood, the Amazon infighter, all hat and right-wing convictions. This certainly didn't apply to those present. Many were MPs' wives, and all of them displayed the nice balance of common sense and femininity for which that breed is noted.'[3]

The inevitable question was 'why was this agreeable type so rare among the Conservative activists?' and the only possible answer seemed to be 'that it is very hard to find a womanly woman who has the time to devote to the job; the result is that most of those who do offer themselves are often what one Minister, hastily cloaking himself in anonymity, described as "dedicated, desiccated battleaxes". Too many of them also have a feminist bee in their extravagant bonnets, while more enlightened thinkers would like to play down the division of the sexes, in politics anyway.'

The number of women standing for Parliament in the Labour and Conservative interests declined between 1955 and 1966. In proportion to voting strength and to their total number of candidates the Liberals were more inclined to choose a woman candidate in 1966 than in 1955, but these women were notably unsuccessful.

Women candidates at post-war General Elections

	Conservative	Labour	Liberal	Other	Total
1945	14 (1)	41 (21)	20 (1)	12 (1)	87
1950	28 (6)	42 (14)	45 (1)	11 (nil)	126
1951	25 (6)	41 (11)	11 (2)	nil	77
1955	32 (10)	43 (14)	14 (nil)	2 (nil)	91
1959	28 (12)	36 (13)	16 (nil)	1 (nil)	81
1964	24 (11)	32 (18)	25 (nil)	9 (nil)	90
1966	21 (13)	30 (13)	20 (nil)	10 (nil)	81

The figures in brackets show the number elected

The party spokesmen have their own explanations for this state of affairs. The Labour Party's usual answer is that more women 'are not available'; the Conservative Central Office is content to blame constituency selection committees who persist in the idea that women make poor candidates and unpopular members, in spite of the example of such sterling members as Dame Pat Hornsby-Smith and Dame Joan Vickers who have held marginal seats for many years.[4]

These explanations hardly seem adequate. Certainly women are not attracted by the inefficiency, archaic ritual and childish filibustering of Parliament; it must also be true that politically minded women are not now attracted to a Parliamentary career which has not only become demanding in terms of time and stamina, but so competitive that they may well have to wait several years before being promoted to a constituency which they can have any hope of winning.[5] Another reason may be that to be chosen as a candidate for the first time a candidate nowadays usually needs to be under thirty, and this works against women, who are likely to be much occupied with small children during this vital decade. Mrs Roy Jenkins, wife of the present Chancellor of the Exchequer, has answered the question 'why are women not more successful in public life?' by saying 'For the excellent reason that most of them put their private lives first and everything else is second. For a woman to become head of a Government department, for example, she must put in as much as a man. But she may have had to sacrifice more.'[6]

In her invaluable book *Women at Westminster*, Pamela Brookes has analysed the family and educational background and the careers of the eighty-three women who have sat in the House of Commons during the half-century following Lady Astor's pioneering assault on this male club. The average age at the time of their first election of the sixty-seven women who have chosen to reveal it is forty-five. Only two—Jennie Lee and Megan Lloyd George—have been under thirty. Only seventeen had children of school age or under when they were elected. Twenty married women and widows were childless. Educationally, their standard has always been high. Only six left school at fourteen or fifteen. Twenty-nine attended a university. Forty of them had served on local government bodies before entering Parliament. The occupations of those declaring a profession were, at the time of election:

Schoolteacher	10
Trade union or political organiser	8

Journalist or writer	6
Farmer, landowner	4
Civil servant	3
Welfare officer	3
Doctor	3
Actress	2
Barrister	2
Company director	2
Secretary	2
Economist	1
Industrial relations consultant	1
State-registered nurse	1
Organising secretary	1
Sociologist	1
University lecturer	1

(A surprising number of the most prominent, Mrs Brookes points out, have had red hair and been small in stature.)

Once selected, however, a woman may have considerable advantages as a Parliamentary candidate. In 1964 *The Times*[7] drew up a balance sheet with which it is hard to disagree.

'She may not be able to visit pubs and clubs as freely as a man, but on the other hand she is more readily invited to address women's organisations, contribute to women's columns in the press, open bazaars and fêtes; moreover, she attracts greater publicity than a man. Opponents seldom pull their punches in dealing with her, but when it is seen that she can return these punches with knowledge and wit, people are duly impressed.

'Women make good listeners, and voters will confide in them very easily. Contrary to popular belief the ability to listen, as well as to speak, is an important attribute of the successful candidate and Member.

'But women can be effective speakers, the more so because they often have the ability to explain complex matters in simple, easily understood language, and can communicate with people otherwise unmoved by high-flown oratory.'

Seated within Parliament, however, it has often been difficult for women to feel that their talents have been adequately or sensibly used. On 5 March 1942, Dr Edith Summerskill told the House that she was tired of serving on committees on which men had been appointed to deal with questions affecting women. 'I am beginning to feel,' she said, 'that the war is being prosecuted by both sexes and directed by one.' There had been a particularly absurd instance of this a few weeks previously, when the Government had proposed to appoint an all-male committee to enquire into allegations of immorality in the women's services. Mrs Thelma Cazalet-Keir therefore asked if 'it would be a good thing to set up an all-woman committee to enquire into conditions in the male services?' The Government then changed its mind and appointed a new committee of five women and three men, with a woman chairman.

There is probably a belief among most Conservatives, if not among most supporters of the Liberal and Labour parties, that women are happier and more useful as candidates' wives than as candidates, but the recent habit of interviewing wives and husbands together has aroused the furious opposition of feminists. This boiled over in 1964[8] when the three men on the Conservative short list for the East Grinstead by-election were summoned to present themselves to the divisional Conservative Association's council together with their wives. This Noah's ark ordeal took place on the stage of the Whitehall Ballroom, East Grinstead. Members of the divisional council put to them any questions that seemed relevant and the final choice was then made by ballot.

East Grinstead was a coveted safe seat and the vacancy had been caused by the elevation to the House of Lords of the former Member, Mrs Evelyn Emmet. There were three candidates, Geoffrey Johnson Smith, aged forty, formerly MP for Holborn and St Pancras; Geoffrey Rippon, aged forty, Minister of Public Building & Works in the last Government, and David

Crouch, aged forty-five, a marketing and advertising consultant. Mrs Ann Rippon protested against what she felt to be an embarrassing occasion and her feelings were fully supported by Vera Brittain in a strong letter to *The Times*.[9] East Grinstead, she said, had been guilty of an outrageous piece of anti-feminism, which 'every woman in public life will surely deplore'. This kind of procedure, she insisted, 'reduces a wife to the status of a mere appendage—unless, of course, she is to be legally allocated a proportion of her husband's parliamentary salary.' How, also, would this practice, if it became general, affect the position of the women MPs, recently an exceptionally lively and promising group? 'Are their husbands to be summoned for interviews too, and can one imagine, for example, Mr Ted Castle or the late Mr Aneurin Bevan submitting to such an ordeal? It is to be sincerely hoped that the East Grinstead basis of selection will not constitute a precedent.' The Conservative Central Office produced an uneasy but soothing answer—the women's vote is an extremely important matter—and the practice quietly continues. The fortunate candidate at East Grinstead, incidentally, was Mr Geoffrey Johnson Smith.

Although on local councils women hold a much larger proportion of the seats than they do in the Commons, it is only in London, in some of the larger cities, and in a few counties and boroughs in the south of England that they are found in considerable numbers. In March 1965 nearly one-third of the members of the London County Council were women, and in ten out of thirteen of the main committees of the council women were either chairmen or vice-chairmen.[10]

No woman has yet been Lord Mayor of London. Of the ninety-six Lord Mayors of Birmingham to date all have been men; Leeds, however has had five women. An enquiry among councillors, carried out by the *Birmingham Sunday Mercury*, found that 'one of the chief male arguments in favour of the *status quo* was the doubt that a woman would be physically strong enough to carry out the year's exhausting round of engagements.'[11] The women, not surprisingly, thought this was rubbish. Alderman Mrs Smith told the reporter that there were at least half a dozen women on the council 'who could walk this job'. She thought the physical objection was a red herring and she was sure that many of the women on the council worked harder than the men. She realised that a man had to earn his living, as well as carry out his council work, but quite often he had leave of absence from his job and then went back and picked up where he had left off. A woman on the other hand still had to catch up with her housework when she reached home after council meetings. Women proved they could do this, and she was sure that the right woman would stand the strain of the top job. 'Anyway,' she added, 'we've had some rather delicate men as Lord Mayors.'

Councillor Mrs Cooke knew perfectly well that Birmingham was very much a man's city and always had been. But, in her view, only experience and seniority were relevant when choosing a Lord Mayor, not the sex of the candidate. 'As women members of the council, we are expected to work on a level footing with the men. We do the same jobs. We don't ask for privileges.' Yet, even so, this hesitation about supporting a woman for Lord Mayor persisted. Mrs Cooke did not agree with the frequent objection that many of the Lord Mayor's engagements were all-male affairs at which a woman's attendance might be embarrassing. 'I have spoken to all-male groups both in this country and in America without any difficulties,' she told the paper.

Alderman F. F. Griffin, leader of the Conservative group, said he had no prejudice at all against women, but 'one has to recognise that generally men are trained from school-leaving age to do certain tasks and because of their acquired skills have aptitudes in certain directions that women lack. And I do not say that in any derogatory sense.' Alderman Victor Turton (Labour) thought that having a woman Lord Mayor would exclude the civic leader from many male functions. 'They would not want to attend stag functions—and the men wouldn't want them anyway,' and he added with Birmingham frankness, 'there is still a certain amount of prejudice against a woman holding the office purely because she is a woman.' Councillor Anthony Beaumont Dark (Conservative) said he would be against having a woman Lord Mayor. A man would be better, 'because it's a man's world'. But he generously admitted that he was very much in favour of women on the City Council. 'They do a magnificent job.'

There was also comment from a former woman member of the council, Dame Edith Pitt, MP for Edgbaston and former Parliamentary Secretary at the Ministry of Health. Dame Edith said that she was unable to believe that there wasn't a woman on the council 'good enough to take the responsibility and discharge this job with dignity'. 'Quite frankly,' she went on, 'I would have loved to have done it myself. But I remember one city councillor who told me: "In your presence Edith, over my dead body will a woman ever be Lord Mayor of this city!" '

The north-east is traditionally a male-dominated part of the country, too. People who move there from the south often find the persistence of the Andy Capp mentality oppressive and it certainly helps to give a nineteenth-century flavour to the area. This has been recognised by officials who have the difficult job of persuading southerners that the north-east is booming, modern, and a good place to live and work in. Speaking at a meeting in Durham in 1963, John Iles, a Londoner in charge of the North East Regional Organisation at the Ministry of Housing, asserted that the north-east was 'too much of a masculine community.'[12] He said he 'would like to see the women taking the men by the nose'. One example of masculine influence which offended him professionally was the lack of consideration of women which was shown when designing houses. Another sign of what he called 'the north-east's masculinity' was the fact that women were barred from entering certain rooms in hotels. That was nonsense. 'We must recognise the women's influence,' he insisted, 'so that people who are already in the north-east want to stay here, and people from other parts of the country want to move in.'

The public bodies with the worst record so far as the representation of women is concerned are the Regional Economic Advisory Councils. When the membership of the first three councils was announced in February 1965 it was immediately noted that out of the 127 members only one was a woman. The chairmen of the councils, *The Guardian* believed, 'delude themselves if they think—as they appear to think—that civic wisdom resides exclusively in men. The practice of local government has proved, time and again and in all parts of the country, that the balance of advantage (not to mention the balance of intelligence) rests with a council with women members.'[13] The last point is well known, if not well publicised, by town clerks and other permanent council officials. Women members of local councils are in general more intelligent and better educated than their male colleagues; without their presence, the mental level of many council debates and committees would be a great deal lower than it is.

By the spring of 1966, however, when the new Regional Councils had all been established, the position was no better. A letter to *The Times*[14] from fourteen women's organisations pointed out that in a total of 300 members there were only four women. This they felt was 'inadequate representation for half the community, a half moreover deeply concerned with the economic and social needs of the areas in which they live.' The letter revealed that a deputation which met the Minister during the setting up of the Regional Councils pressed the particular contribution which women could make, not only individually, but through the national women's organisations. After the meeting three names were submitted from a joint committee of women's organisations, but the deputation's advice appeared to have been disregarded. When the Planning Council for the South East was announced, the nearly forty members included only one woman—and her appointment seemed to result simply from the fact that she was chairman of the Greater London Council Housing Committee.

'It cannot be accepted,' the letter continued, 'that women are not willing to serve in these capacities. Experience shows that women can play an able and constructive role in local government, the magistracy, the social services, and now increasingly in the government of this country. We are left wondering what qualifications are chiefly looked for in appointing members to these councils; how vacancies will be filled in the future and what constitutes an acceptable recommending body.'

A careful examination of the names and qualifications of the councils' members, and a closer knowledge of one of them, suggests why so few women were appointed. The emphasis is on people with experience and local power in the fields of economics, planning, transport, trade-union work and finance, all of them areas in which the influence of women is small. Rightly or wrongly, the chairmen of the councils appear to have seen their primary task as being that of mapping out the ground and drawing up a quantitative plan. Their reports, or at least those which have so far appeared, have much to say about such economically important matters as population increase, potential growth points and transport densities, employment categories and income statistics, but remarkably little about the quality of life in the cities, villages and towns in the Regions. This may have been a correct order of priority, but to at least one reader the result has been reports of extraordinary dullness and of equally extraordinary abstraction and lack of human interest and reality. They are hardly the kind of documents that could have appeared if the councils had had a 50 per cent women membership; but, on the other hand, the briefing given to the councils may have made their singularly unexciting and very worthy all-male membership inevitable.

In many forms of public activity one senses the feeling that Lord Cecil so honestly expressed in Parliament before the first world war, that once women are admitted the whole atmosphere changes and life will never be the same again. This kind of conservatism, which women inevitably see as anti-feminism, is still very noticeable in legal circles (where incidentally membership of the Freemasons is extremely large. The proportion of judges, barristers, solicitors and high-ranking police officers who are Freemasons is probably higher than for any other occupational group in the country, not excluding bank managers and regular Service officers).

The achievement of Mrs Elizabeth Lane in becoming the first woman High Court Judge is therefore all the more remarkable and epoch-making. It followed close on the appointment of Miss Edna Cann as the first woman town clerk.[15] *The Solicitors' Journal*[16] commented on certain consequences of the appointment of Mrs Lane to the Probate, Divorce & Admiralty Division of the High Court. It noted that there had been argument as to the correct way of addressing Mrs Lane and concluded, 'Whatever may have been the custom when Judge Lane has been sitting as a divorce commissioner, we think the time has come to be really radical. Why should she not be called "Mrs Justice Lane" and addressed as "Your Ladyship"? Unmarried female judges in the future would be "Miss" instead of "Mrs". There will undoubtedly be more female judges as time goes on and it would be a good idea to start logically. Equally we could settle once and for all the objection to the title "Dame" by substituting "Lady", which would please a large number of ladies who do not like being called dames.'

With the walls of tradition breached, if not actually down, and a woman presiding in the High Court, it will surely become less possible to preserve the anti-feminist fiction that certain kinds of legal evidence are not for female eyes or ears, a pretence that many women magistrates find a great deal more embarrassing than the evidence itself.

Some photographs produced in court are unquestionably unpleasant, and a sensitive, inexperienced person, whether man or woman, might well be greatly disturbed by seeing them. Nowadays new magistrates are fortunately compelled to attend courses to prepare them for their duties, but in most cases such courses are confined to legal matters and to visiting prisons and borstals. It is difficult to provide adequate, relevant lectures on cruelty and perversion, so that the recruit to the bench will be surprised at nothing when the real thing comes along. Human beastliness has to be learnt about slowly and in its context; and for some people the learning process can bring shocks. This may be harder for women than for men, especially where the case involves children, but a magistrate who cannot put emotions aside and take a cool, dispassionate attitude towards the matter in hand is unfitted to the job. It is possible that some women might judge a case more capably if they had not been subjected to an ordeal-by-photograph that was too much for them. A student nurse often faints once or twice when she begins her training in an operating theatre; but she is no help until she overcomes this stage, and she has to build her own defences against what she must look at. Nobody else can toughen her, and the same holds good for magistrates. If, through male protectiveness, women magistrates are never to be allowed to see unpleasant things, how is the toughening—and equalising—process ever to begin?

Not infrequently patriarchal judges carry this protectiveness to absurd lengths. In 1967, the London firm of Calder & Boyars was prosecuted under the Obscene Publications Act for publishing *Last Exit to Brooklyn*. The jury at the Central Criminal Court was all male. Judge Graham Rogers, who said he had read the book, directed that there should be no women on the jury, 'as they might be embarrassed at having to read a book which dealt with homosexuality, prostitution, sadism, drug-taking and sexual perversion.'[17] One of *The Times*'s men readers was sufficiently provoked by this to suggest that logic demanded that in future juries considering abortion cases should be wholly composed of women.[18] Miss Dee Wells was even more scathing: 'Sex being the two-sex activity it usually is, it seems a pity to have excluded women from a jury that will deal with almost nothing but,' and she doubted if women were as easily embarrassed as men. In any case, she added, 'I'm not at all sure that most men know enough about sex, or take what they know seriously enough, to provide, on their own, the best balance for such a job.'[19]

One recalls that there was no woman on the jury in 1923 when Dr Marie Stopes brought a libel action against Dr Halliday Sutherland, who had attacked her teaching. Dr Stopes lost her case. The proceedings were dominated by the prevalent male view that female ignorance was right and proper, that contraception, if undertaken at all, was the responsibility of men and that the divine destiny of the poor was to breed. There was, however, a significant difference between the situation in 1923 and today. When Dr Sutherland gained his victory, he was supported by many women doctors. Nowadays, male obscurantism finds little encouragement from this particular quarter.

Two ludicrous instances of judicial prudery took place in the year before the *Last Exit to Brooklyn* case. At the beginning of a case involving rape, Mr Justice James said at Nottinghamshire Assizes that any ladies present might wish to leave.[20] It so happened that in the public gallery was a class of girls from Boots College of Further Education, Nottingham, visiting as part of their education. The girls remained seated and the Judge said he could not compel them to leave. Some women in the public seats then left the court and the Judge said: 'I see the ladies present have left.' The girls, who were aged seventeen and eighteen, eventually left after an usher had spoken to their teacher, Mr Michael Pestell. Mr Pestell said afterwards: 'I did not think the case would be embarrassing to the girls. They are all teenagers and work in Boots. I have been with them before to the assizes when such cases have been heard, but have never been asked to leave.'

The following month, twenty-nine girls from a Swedish high school left an Appeal Court after Lord Parker, the Lord Chief Justice, had spoken to the English teacher who was in charge of the party. Lord Parker's argument was that if the girls remained, 'It would make it very difficult to present the case properly in the detail it should be.' The case in question concerned alleged indecency between men. The girls accordingly left and went to other courts.[21] One of two teachers with the party commented: 'Most of the girls here will be going on to university. They have all received sex instruction in school, and I do not think they would be shocked by anything they heard here. They are all little ladies. I think, perhaps you are a little . . .' The teacher could not think of the word in English, but agreed with the reporter that the word 'unenlightened' would express what she had in mind.

The keep-women-out rules of London's West End clubs created no problems so long as the public and professional institutions wishing to meet there were run entirely by men, and so long as the clubs were sufficiently prosperous not to trouble with accommodating profitable functions arranged by other bodies. Nowadays, however, there can be real problems causing distress and humiliation as correspondence to *The Times* in 1964 revealed.

'When the professional association to which I belong was being entertained by a public board at a Pall Mall Club,' wrote Mrs Margherita Rendel, 'I was turned away on the steps, while my (male) colleagues were being welcomed in. I am sure that if such a thing had happened to a member of a minority group—for example, had a coloured person been turned away in such circumstances—there would have been a public outcry. One would think that the community would resent equally discrimination against women.'[22]

Mrs Barbara Garden, of Dewsbury, reported an equally unpleasant occasion, its conclusion almost weird. 'Like Margherita Rendel I arrived at the steps of an all-male club to be told by the door-man that ladies were never allowed to mount them or to enter. I pointed out that they had accepted my entrance money for the meeting which was to be held there and for which I had made the journey to London, also they had been kind enough to arrange overnight accommodation for me.

As I had signed all the correspondence with my full name they knew I was not Santa Claus; and I therefore requested that they decide, and quickly, how my entrance was to be made. My male colleagues were getting impatient when the man said: "If you will go round the corner, round the second, and then round the third, I will come and escort you upstairs." Round the bend I went—three times; the door was there and very clearly labelled: "LADIES AND BAGGAGE".'[23]

Mrs Garden's attitude was found unreasonable by a male correspondent from Bromley.

'What, if anything, is wrong with men associating under the exclusive aegis of a Pall Mall club or any like institution? It seems to me quite in order that ladies should be excluded if that is a rule of the club, and, if your correspondent wishes to be entertained by a public board, she should indicate to the donor of the invitation that she may be excluded from the place of venue. Also, of course, it is the duty of the donor not to issue an invitation which cannot be accepted for this reason, but I don't understand why the club should be obliged to change its rules.'[24]

An even more ludicrous anomaly occurs each year at the Royal Academy annual dinner, from which women academicians and associates are barred, no matter how great their eminence.[25] The chairman of the Fawcett Society, Mrs Thelma Cazalet Keir, drew attention to this idiocy after the dinner held in April 1965. The President, she noted, 'welcomed the presence of Mr Mellon among his guests and publicly thanked both him and his wife for lending for exhibition their very lovely collection of English paintings. He then expressed gratitude for the beautiful collection of seventeenth-century Dutch paintings and of English silver lent by Mrs Assheton-Bennet. Finally he announced that among forthcoming exhibitions there would be one in the Diploma Gallery of the works of that distinguished Royal Academician—Dame Laura Knight.'[26] Dame Laura was not, of course, present.

Such antique nonsense continues to be encouraged at Oxford and Cambridge dinners, despite hard-won concessions in other departments of university life. In 1964, for instance, a proposal arose to admit women to formal dinners at Christ Church, Oxford.[27] Mr Mario Cerutti, president of the Junior Common Room, announced that the proposal would not be forwarded for approval by the governing body in view of 'a solid block of resentment and hostility'. This could make it 'very unpleasant' for any woman dining in college and wreck it as a social occasion. At present the only woman admitted to formal dinners is the Queen, the college's Visitor. The Queen, like cloakroom attendants and barmaids in men-only bars, is traditionally regarded as sexless.

Women on the serving side of bars are one thing, but in Britain it is felt necessary to emphasise by every possible means that, as customers, men are in pubs and bars as of right and women on sufferance. At least one pub in Leeds has a notice over the bar saying that women are asked not to crowd round the bar, in order to allow men to order their drinks. Such a notice would be less likely, if not unthinkable, in the south, but all over Britain there is a very strong resistance to the recurrent suggestion that pubs should be turned into places where whole families may relax and refresh themselves. The Consumer Council has demanded that pubs should be open in the afternoons, sell tea, coffee and snacks and allow parents to bring their children; and it has submitted these proposals to the Monopolies Commission. Miss Elizabeth Ackroyd, the Council's director, has said that 'pubs are for beer' is the essence of the brewers' outlook.[28] This was thought fair enough for people who wanted it that way, but not everyone did, particularly families who liked eating and drinking together when out. Miss Ackroyd felt that the traditional British pub should by all means be preserved, but not as the only thing between the restaurant which can just serve drinks with meals, and the club which can serve anything it likes at any time.

'Why,' asked Jean Steant, 'are the publicans and the puritans so frightened of allowing children into the pubs?' and concluded that it was just a male plot. 'The laws are nothing to do with the times when children would be sent round for a jugful of gin and stagger home half intoxicated. It's just that men don't want to be bothered with the kids (and often the wife) around and it's the easiest way of keeping them all out.'[29]

While on the subject of drink, one might note that there is a firmly entrenched British attitude that knowing about wine is an exclusively male talent. Women are erroneously supposed to like nothing but sweet, preferably sparkling, white wines and, equally fatuously, to have been born without the ability to distinguish a good wine from a poor one. Mr Edmund Penning-Rowsell has suggested that 'knowing about wine' is the last refuge of masculine superiority.[30] This, he thinks, may be 'partly a relic of the days when *the* wine was vintage port, and the ladies were sent packing to the drawing-room while the gentlemen got down to the real business of the evening. In view of the assumed preference of women for sweet wine, I have always thought it a little hard that they were not solaced upstairs with a bottle of fine sauternes, while down below the men sank into semi-stupor and total obscenity. It may yet be women who will lead us back to a proper appreciation of sauternes, so often undervalued and mislabelled today.' He believes that the assumption that women like white and sweet wines may often be no more than a male cover-up for personal preferences they are ashamed to admit, and considers it both curious and significant that women have never been encouraged to acquire a taste for vintage port, one of the sweetest of all wines. His experience, he reveals, 'is that women who have been encouraged rather than discouraged in the matter of wine very often have much better and, equally important, more objective judgment than men.' Their opinion is not distorted by a famous name or a fashionable vintage.

A self-defence organisation, the Women's Wine Club, an offshoot of the Directors' Wine Club, was established in 1967 and has premises in Bond Street. 'Taste, like temperament, cuts clean across the sex barrier,' claims the club's introductory letter, and it has no time for the old-world militant-suffragette attitude. Its simple aim is advising women who like wine but may be diffident about asking for advice on the subject. There is absolutely no mystique about the Club at all, and no attempt to make it snobbish or exclusive. The subscription is only 10s a year; the list of wines available is short, to the point, and includes brief and helpful descriptions of each item.[31]

The Writers' & Press Club, originally the Women's Press Club, was another British organisation started by women in self-defence, and was the only women's press club in the world.

During the second world war when correspondents, who were at that time 80 per cent women and 20 per cent men, came back to London after a day's press facility in the provinces, the men went off to the all-male Press Club to eat: everywhere else was shut and the women went hungry. In 1943 a dozen of them founded the club in Carey Street, meals being the most important activity, both for themselves and as an opportunity to interview famous people. The club closed in March 1968 as a result of rising expenses.

The Association of Women Shareholders was set up in 1964 to help women with their investments, but since then has had a curious history. After a year it was discovered that the association had been conquered by infiltration: male members outnumbered women by three to one. The organisers decided to accept the situation and formed a new company, Investors & Shareholders Association, to take over the old one. It was not known how all these men had found their way on to the books of an organisation created specifically to help women. Many of them had probably been goaded into applying on behalf of their wives, who were either too shy to write themselves or felt that, despite the Association's name, investment remained very much a man's world. Another likely theory is that the men joined because they reckoned that the Association gave them access to exceptionally honest and practical advice of a kind not easily obtainable from the traditional male-orientated, male-run institutions.

Some banks have toyed with the idea of opening branches specially designed for the supposedly distinctive needs and tastes of women customers and one, the National Commercial Bank of Scotland, has actually done so, in Princes Street, Edinburgh, after one of the directors had seen and admired the Ladies' Bank in Auckland, New Zealand.[32] It has 'a feminine manager, accountant and staff of four in white nylon overalls with their names embroidered on the pocket in blue silk. The entrance hall is carpeted in olive green and flanked by walls papered in gold and white on one side and with gold leather cloth on the other. Business will be transacted, with coffee to refresh the shopping-weary customers, at a teak counter with a mirrored base to give a spacious effect and to reflect back the carpet area. Ceilings of natural spruce, black leathercloth chairs and shell-pink fittings in a beautifully appointed powder room complete the static décor. Curtains and flowers add the finishing touches.' A banking atmosphere which many men, too, would greatly appreciate. Here every woman can cash up to £10 whatever her home branch, without any checking or query; the directors say that it would be impossible to consider extending that service to men. Most bank managers would agree with this point of view, accepting that women are more basically honest and more worried about not getting into debt—although one cynic has suggested that it is about time 'they learned how to do so'.

Other banks have nibbled at the idea of a special approach to their women customers, usually by means of rather patronising and childishly written little booklets. The directors of the National Commercial Bank of Scotland are exceptional in emphasising that they want to treat women as equals with men, with equal money rights and equal financial understanding—which seems, in 1967, a fairly obvious thing to do.

Bastion after bastion has failed during the 1960s, but the battles have almost invariably been ferocious. The male garrisons have yielded with a minimum of willingness and grace and nowhere has the battle been fought more fiercely than at the Jockey Club. In 1966, Mrs Florence Nagle, a successful trainer, was refused a trainer's licence on grounds of her sex. The stewards had to give way after Mrs Nagle had successfully sued them. But as a proviso attached to the licence, counsel for the Jockey Club produced this masterpiece.

'Your client will doubtless appreciate that in the realm of horse racing there are many who are known to be, or to associate with, undesirable persons, but in regard to whom no proof of such undesirability could be established. The Stewards, particularly in matters of security, are often obliged to rely, as indeed are the police, upon information which they cannot disclose, obtained from sources which they cannot reveal, if they are to continue to be supplied with information. It is for this reason that the grant or withdrawal of licences has been entrusted solely to the Stewards who are, of course, under a duty to members of the Jockey Club to exercise their powers honestly and for the benefit of horse racing.

'Were our clients now to grant to your client a licence, such a decision in the present context could doubtless be regarded as an admission that the Stewards do not have the unfettered discretion, whether the applicant be male or female, which is essential if they are properly to discharge their functions. In such circumstances it would be only a matter of time before our clients had to face further litigation. In these circumstances our clients are prepared, in view of the advice which they have received, to grant to your client the licence for which she has recently applied provided she expressly acknowledges that the licence was granted by the Stewards in the exercise of their absolute and unfettered discretion. In view of the publicity these proceedings have received there would have to be an agreed statement in court, and this could doubtless be agreed between counsel.'[33]

So the stewards gave way on condition that Mrs Nagle publicly acknowledged that they were her masters. This defensive strategy surely represents the ultimate in sophistry, a quality much in evidence throughout the longstanding resistance movement to extension of women's rights.

What kind of summary can be attempted of the success of the efforts women have made in the post-war years to secure themselves a more adequate position in public life? One kind of answer is provided by the list of birthdays of prominent people published each day in *The Times*. During six consecutive days in 1964 a total of sixty-four men and four women received recognition; for another period of six days in 1965 there were sixty-four men and seven women. During 1966 and 1967 spot checks on the new-style *Times* under the editorship of Mr William Rees-Mogg showed that in this respect it did no better than under the less with-it rule of Sir William

Men and Women

Haley: as public figures, men are reckoned to be roughly ten times as interesting as women, or are ten times more often of a status *The Times* considers worthy of notice. Where women are mentioned in *The Times*'s lists, they are likely to be actresses, novelists or bearers of titles acquired as a result of marriage.

SEVEN

The Femininity Problem

The question has been many times put.[1] Why are there so few women television interviewers, particularly in programmes of the 'Face to Face' type, where the very personal nature of the interview might have been thought attractive and fruitful for women? Is the male monopoly in such work mere tradition and prejudice, or is there some better reason? Two women with extensive experience of television have given their own answers to this.[2]

Eleanor Bron's view was: 'There is something not neutral about a woman. Men in their presence tend to be either chivalrous or flirtatious. This tends to elicit a phoney response from men. Viewers accept a man's interviewing as a more natural condition.

'There is also a kind of forthrightness and aggressiveness needed for good TV which is not particularly feminine; women to be attractive have to be conciliatory, but this is not the best way to elicit responses on TV. She can't use the true arts of a woman for getting responses, which is to be gentle, sympathetic and understanding. If the programme is about politics then the interviewer must be tough; an audience feels threatened and put upon. It's not natural for her to be doing it.'

Joan Bakewell, an interviewer for 'Late Night Line-up', thought that this argument applied only to TV programmes controversial in theme. 'I don't think I would be given an interview job that demanded a muscular, tough relentless

Notes to this chapter are on page 178

attitude on the part of the interviewer. It's more difficult for a woman to be rude on TV. But I don't think interviews have to be aggressive to be successful.

'I don't want to be a cipher on the box. I hope people will think I have attitudes. But women are emotive objects and if a woman feels something she tends to express it very intensely. This might annoy men, who hate losing an argument to a woman on TV. It looks like an act of sexual aggression if a woman tries to win an argument and that's why it would be difficult to have a female Robin Day on the screen.'

In Britain experiments with women newsreaders have been considered unsuccessful, both in television and on radio, mainly for the reason given by Miss Bakewell, that women find it difficult to keep hints of their personal feelings out of their presentation of the news. This matters only so long as a non-personal style of reading is reckoned essential. There are signs, however, that this particular tradition may be on the way out and that the involved newsreader, the journalist who broadcasts his own material and comments on it as he goes along, may be accepted for the 1970s. Women journalists might well be more effective in such a framework, happy to make it clear, by the expression on their face or by the tone in their voice, that they believe this public figure has said something dubious or that someone else deserves respect. Interviewing may be another matter, however. If a woman wins an argument with a man, or forces him to say what is really in his mind, she must, it appears, lose some degree of femininity in the process, and one wonders how many women are prepared to face this, or for how long viewers would tolerate it.

This has been considered from a different angle by Lord Mancroft, a Conservative barrister in his mid-fifties, with a son and four daughters. In a *Times* interview he welcomes women in public life, but thinks they should be judged on their ability, not their sex. 'Listening to Parliament in session I notice only whether members are argumentative or noisy—not whether they are men or women behaving like this. In the same way I would consider that Shirley Williams was one of the most able of the newer MPs of either sex. Pat Hornsby-Smith in her day did her work as well as, if not better than, any man, while Joan Vickers, with her blue hair, is a character and seems to hold her seat by sheer force of personality.

'But however effective a woman politician is, I think it is essential that she should never lose her femininity or become aggressively feminist, ramming opinions down one's throat every five minutes. I agree with almost everything that Edith Summerskill says (except about professional boxing—and I'm sure she'll get her Bill through yet), but she will keep behaving as if she were still in the days of suffragettes. That sometimes puts people against her.'[3]

Lord Mancroft sees some occupations as better suited to women, and some less. He favours women gynaecologists, but would himself 'rather have a man for any doctoring of a personal nature,' although a woman doctor would be perfectly suitable for dealing with, say, a broken leg. He has, in the best British tradition, 'a deep and burning loathing and hatred of seeing men ballet dancers prancing round a stage in tights. That, too, should be left to women.' But he recognises certain natural disadvantages from which women suffer. 'In theory women barristers have exactly the same opportunities as men, but that is not quite true. Solicitors tend to avoid briefing a feminine barrister unless she is exceptional. And even though they may be absolutely brilliant academically, in court women can often be difficult to hear because their voices are light and high-pitched. Of course there are those who have triumphed like Rose Heilbron, who is a QC, and Elizabeth Lane, now a judge; one has overcome her natural liability, and the other has a deep, almost masculine voice.'

The pitch of the voice apart, it is not easy for a woman to achieve a style of speaking which is acceptable to mixed audiences, or to gatherings of men. If she is over-colloquial she is liable to be thought unfeminine, and if she is under-colloquial she will be accused of being pedantic. Men get away with an appalling degree of pomposity and cliché;

women are expected to be 'natural'. As after-dinner speakers men all too often receive a rapturous welcome for inanities, because both they and their audiences have had too much to drink. This is not the kind of occasion at which women excel. They are looked at more when they speak in public, both by men and by women; the interest given to their person and their clothes distracts attention from what they are trying to say. The more 'feminine' their appearance is—and a judge's wig and robes, like a cookery demonstrator's overall, are a great help in disguising femininity—the less effective their remarks are likely to be.

Another difficult and controversial field for women trying to combine efficiency with femininity is the ownership and driving of cars. The classic James Bond view expresses what many men feel about this. 'Women are often meticulous and safe drivers, but they are very seldom first-class. In general Bond regarded them as a mild hazard and he always gave them plenty of road and was ready for the unpredictable. Four women in a car he regarded as the highest potential danger, and two women nearly as lethal. Women together cannot keep silent in a car, and when women talk they have to look into each other's faces. An exchange of words is not enough. They have to see the other person's expression, perhaps in order to read behind the other's words or to analyse the reaction to their own. So two women in the front seat of a car constantly distract each other's attention from the road ahead and four women are more than doubly dangerous, for the driver not only has to hear, and see, what her companion is saying, but also, for women are like that, what the two behind are talking about.

'But this girl drove like a man. She was entirely focused on the road ahead and on what was going on in her driving mirror, an accessory rarely used by women except for making up their faces. And, equally rare in a woman, she took a man's pleasure in the feel of her machine, in the timing of her gear changes, and the use of her brakes.'[4]

The observation is shrewd, but did the fact that the exceptional girl 'drove like a man' make her less desirable in Bond's eyes? Did her driving ability reduce her femininity? The answer is to be found elsewhere in the novel.

So long as women drivers were a small minority, it was possible for the press to treat them as a stock joke, like mothers-in-law, and for the manufacturers to think of them as accessories who sat in cars without driving them. Even now, and despite the large number of women drivers, British car manufacturers continue to give the impression of believing that the greatest, if not the only, influence women should have on car design is on colour. Colour is felt to be feminine —give a woman a prettily coloured car and she'll be happy. Yet Frances Howell, one of two women members of the Guild of Motoring Writers, carried out her own private survey, untrammelled by the prejudices of the manufacturers and motoring press, and discovered women attached little importance to colour, that they did not in fact like two-tone cars—supposed to have been provided with them in mind —and that they liked plain upholstery.

'Surely the truth is that women don't especially want cars designed for women—at least not if it simply means prettily coloured ones. They just want well-designed, efficient machines. The practical considerations women are interested in are cars that one can get in and out of easily; driving seats that push forward without brute force, handbrakes that can be secured without the grip of an all-in wrestler; foot pedals designed for size five high heels rather than size ten brogues; and more safety, especially for children. We are still waiting for the wheel that can be changed by a woman. It's not lack of knowledge that's holding us back, as most men prefer to think, just a flat refusal to cope with a job that female logic tells us could be made easier.'[5]

The manufacturers have a problem here. Most women, sensibly, want a car that is convenient, practical and reliable. Many, if not most, men approach motoring differently, whether or not they identify their own feelings: a car, for them, is a mettlesome horse, to be tamed and ridden and understood. A journey is a challenge, a struggle to prove themselves against the road, the elements, the mechanical quirks of the car and other road users. It becomes, then, almost feminine to want no more of a car than that it should get one easily from place to place. Manufacturers of many kinds are slow to realise the potential market for equipment—for instance grass-cutters and mechanical cultivators—which can be comfortably used by women.

Recruiting advertisements for the Services and the police have to handle the femininity question warily. The feminine woman and the woman bursting with leadership-qualities and longing to make decisions tend to be rather different people. The marriage is achieved in this way: 'WHO SAYS A GIRL CAN'T MAKE DECISIONS?

'As an officer in the Women's Royal Army Corps you prove (in a very feminine way, of course) that a woman can handle responsibility just as well as men. You work alongside men; yet you make your own decisions, issue instructions, as an executive in your own right. But the life you lead doesn't mean you have to sacrifice any of your femininity—your accommodation, for instance, and your uniform are designed for modern women in a modern age.'[6]

Apart from the awkward fact that few women believe absolute obedience to authority—the supreme military virtue —to be acceptable or good for the character, the difficulty is of course, that making your own decisions and issuing instructions are still considered by most British people to be nearly as unfeminine as science.

One woman with a good deal of experience of industry and commerce who holds a responsible executive position has admitted that she finds herself 'claiming the treatment of a man in the day-time and the treatment of a woman in the evening.'[7] Business women, she feels, can be divided into two camps. 'The first are those who attempt to ape men, whose clothes become square cut, whose voices become loud, who learn to swear and to drink; I used to think that these women existed only in the minds of businessmen but having met a large number myself I am now compelled to acknowledge their existence. The second category is that of the strictly female female who makes blatant use of her femininity and of her over-played "weakness" to achieve her aims. It is very seldom that you find a woman attempting to fight fair once she has entered the bastions of the business world.'

The trouble is that new stereotypes are all the time growing up while people are doing their best to conform to the old ones. This or that attitude is asserted to be incontrovertibly and permanently feminine, on the basis of evidence that has existed for decades or centuries, and then women step forward and announce that the stereotype is rubbish, that they are new women who have shaken off their chains and that they simply don't feel or think the way the stereotype says they do.

An excellent example of this change of attitude concerns jewellery, of which all women are supposed to be passionately fond, and especially diamonds. To possess diamonds we have always been assured that ninety-nine women out of a hundred would do nearly anything. In 1962 the great diamond concern, De Beers, carried out a survey on the jewellery-owning habits of British women.[8] They revealed that the average woman in Britain owns thirteen pieces of jewellery. Diamonds are the main feature in eighty-three out of every hundred engagement rings, but while many women own five pairs of ear-rings, one woman in every hundred does not own any jewellery at all. Much more serious for De Beers, they found that cars, holidays and kitchen equipment were much more important to women than diamonds; they concluded that diamonds needed hard selling.

Another widely believed myth is that women, unlike men, are not sexually excited by what they see and that, for them, touch is everything. The Beatles and Mr Swen Swenson, the male stripper from Iowa, should have disposed of this mistaken idea. Mr Swenson is considered a great artist.

'He scarcely takes off a thing. He discards his jacket, then his tie, and finally, as if they were as essential as a G-string, his two red elastic armbands.

'But I have yet to find the woman who hasn't squealed like a Beatle fan at the very mention of him. "He's the sexiest thing I've ever seen on the stage," shrilled one young matron. "He's fabulous—wow!" exclaimed the girl sitting next to me. "I don't know what it is he's up to, but *that's* for me," said a middle-aged woman in the row behind.'[9]

The international argument over topless bathing suits during 1964 produced similar shocks and revelations. Topless women were arrested on French beaches and warned off English ones. The press controversy included a learned biological contribution from Dr C. B. Goodheart, who noted that the female breasts, or rather the nipples, function as what biologists call releasers of feeling and that for men 'sexual releasers are largely visual. Men can be aroused not only by the sight of beautiful women in the flesh but also by their pictures. Magazines for men abound in illustrations of attractive women, usually unclothed, and in these it is the breasts which are emphasised over all other parts of the female anatomy, and sometimes exaggerated to almost pathological proportions. And yet women's magazines are not embellished with comparable pictures of sexually attractive men, nor is there any demand from women for salacious photographs, nor for strip-tease shows and the other sexually stimulating visual entertainments enjoyed by men. This is because the sexual titillation of women, as with all other female primates, is not visual but tactile, in kissing and caressing and so on, and no acceptable substitute for that is to be found in pictorial representation.'[10]

This view was strongly challenged by women who wrote to the *New Scientist* about it. One asked: 'Sir, What about men's nipples and male toplessness—which is now widely practised? Is Mr Goodheart quite sure women are quite "un-visual" in this sense? I think that may be an old bachelor's tale, like women having hardly any sexual feeling at all.'

In the absence of any really authoritative research which would prove or disprove this point, the argument must be left unsettled—with the thought that in 1900 or even in 1920 it would not have been easy for women to have taken part in such a frank exchange of views, except perhaps anonymously. When reading letters of this kind, however, it is difficult to know how much allowance to make for a general feminist determination to prove that the differences between men and women are minimal.

Virginia Woolf insisted many years ago that 'it is fatal for anyone who writes to think of their sex . . . It is fatal for a woman to lay the least stress on any grievance, to plead even with justice in any cause, in any way to speak consciously as a woman.'[11] Jane Austen and Emily Brontë were great because when they were writing they ignored the prejudices of the patriarchal society in which they lived. 'Of all the thousand women who wrote novels then, they almost entirely ignored the perpetual admonitions of the eternal pedagogue—write this, think that. They alone were deaf to that persistent voice, now grumbling, now patronising, now domineering, now grieved, now shocked, now angry, now avuncular, that voice which cannot let women alone, but must be at them, like some too conscientious governess, adjuring them.'[12]

More recently, Brigid Brophy, for instance, has hotly denied that, whatever the fashionable critics may say, there is any specifically feminine quality about novels written by women. If the critic wishes to test this, all he has to do is to read ten novels by men and ten by women without knowing which is which, and correctly attribute them. 'Anyone who can't pass such a test and yet bandies "feminine" as a literary term bandies it without ascertainable meaning attached. And thus it is bandied in literary discussion, where it is now generally agreed that all novels by women possess all the following characteristics and no novels by men possess any of them: emotionalism and cattiness, logic and irrationality, sensibility and earthiness, obsession with detail and romantic slapdashery.'[13]

Miss Storm Jameson, on the other hand, claims to have identified recently a specifically feminine kind of literary genre, to which she has given the no doubt well-deserved label of 'vaginal novels'.[14] Why, she asks, should a talented woman author want to write in this way? 'Why should some of the most intelligent women novelists find interest, pleasure, satisfaction in writing at dreadful length about their or their characters' erotic needs and activities? It is certain that they are not moved by the wish to please; the number of possible readers to whom these variations on a sexual theme give pleasure or amusement must be fairly small, if only because of the relentless solemnity and zeal of Miss X's approach or Miss Y's casually sickening disclosures.' Miss Jameson concludes that these novelists can only be trying to establish a true identity for women, from first principles. Nothing can be assured, no preconceptions are valid. Their hope presumably is that some new vision of womanhood may emerge from a phase of uninhibited searching and analysis. The old mystique must be stripped away, even if there is nothing to replace it.

In this process of delving and laying bare—a process not, of course, confined to women novelists—the old-fashioned quality of glamour, once an essential part of high-grade femininity, has almost vanished. Glamour is necessarily hard to define. Noel Coward, who greatly regrets its disappearance, has tried.[15] 'It is the aura,' he says, 'which used to surround the great female stars on the stage. There are plenty of bloody good actresses about, but very few of them have that indefinable something. I suppose that sex-appeal is part of it. It is almost impossible to describe it completely.'

Nakedness may well kill glamour. As Mae West once said, the woman who needs to take her clothes off in order to prove she has sex-appeal hasn't got any. The same, no doubt, could be said of glamour.

Femininity is a reflection of self-confidence, and for more than twenty years the women's weeklies and monthlies have done their best to inspire women with various kinds of self-confidence, and to weld them together into some kind of movement. The philosophy of the movement, as it has distilled out, is not so different from that of the WRAC advertisement quoted above—what is needed is informed, decision-making femininity, 'modern women in a modern age'. They have, broadly speaking, two aims, to tell women how best to spend their money or, in the advertisers' jargon, 'to create consumer confidence', and to help women towards in the same jargon, 'self-development and self-realisation.'

It has been asserted that three powerful influences are at work among British women today—'detergents, helping them to be clean, Marks & Spencer, helping them to be well dressed, and women's weeklies, keeping them informed.'[16] The influence of these magazines must certainly be considerable. Thirty-four of them are published in Britain, with circulations of 100,000 or over per issue; every week, they are 'read' by two out of three women in the country. Most of them are careful to stay ahead of their readers, but not too far ahead; they lead, but stay well in touch. Whether in new furniture design, or thoughts on dealing with children and husbands, or in ideas for leisure activities, these magazines 'frequently act for the reader in the role of the great confirmer'.[17] They are written specifically for women and in the post-war years they must have done more than any other agency to shape a kind of femininity which makes reasonably good sense to most women, endorsing their own unexpressed feelings. They see women's lives as home-centred, they are rarely outspokenly feminist, and they give little support to the view that the less difference there is between the sexes the better.

They would never, on the other hand, encourage solid reactionary opinions of the Shirley Bassey type. 'Look at that woman who started all the trouble in this country. What's-her-name, Mrs Pankhurst, that woman. "Get back to the kitchen where you belong", some man should have told her. And you know that's what all we women really want. Get put back to the kitchen where we belong. We don't want emancipation.'[18]

The magazines would equally certainly never show signs of agreeing with Miss Bassey's view that 'all women are evil and are to blame for all the evil in the world,' or with the *New Scientist*'s belief—whether *avant-garde* or Genesis-based—that 'the congenital disease known to gynaecologists as the Female Gimmies—gim'me this and gim'me that—is the root of all male misdemeanour.'[19] For the sake of their advertisers, if of nobody else, they would feel obliged to frown on such a cynical piece of anti-feminism as 'the richest men always look harassed because, no matter how much money they make, their ladies always want to spend more. There is no ceiling to the escalation of female desires. Simple men are driven to heave bricks through jewellers' windows so that the acquisitive cries of their birds may be momentarily muffled in furs, but the beaver lamb leads on to the mink stole.'[20]

Their concensus of opinion would more closely reflect the Lord Chancellor's statement to a meeting of magistrates that crime in Britain would decline overnight if men behaved with the same self-discipline and morality as women, and that the fact that British prisons contained thirty men for every one woman proved the point. Their readers would be neither encouraged nor comforted by the Shirley Bassey-*New Scientist* theory that at the centre of femininity was the talent for committing the kind of crime that no government could consider indictable.

Their definition of woman's role in the world would not be unlike that described by the Queen in her 1966 Christmas broadcast. 'It has been women who have breathed gentleness and care into the harsh progress of mankind. The struggles against inhuman prejudice, against squalor, ignorance and disease, have always owed a great deal to the determination and tenacity of women. The devotion of nuns and nurses, the care of mothers and wives, the services of teachers, and the conviction of reformers are the real and enduring presents which women have always given. In the modern world the opportunities for women to give something of value to the human family are greater than ever, because through their own efforts they are now beginning to play their full part in public life.'

Some editors and publishers have seen a ready-made, if minority, market for the more robust newspaper or magazine that plays down femininity. *Nova*, for instance, announced its issue of October 1965 as 'a further development in the campaign to give women a magazine that treats them as people and not as a separate species'. Early in the 1960s *The Guardian* took the view that many women were fed up with being treated as high-level domestic animals and began to seek readers in a more up-to-date fashion. A typical advertisement put the case in this way:

'There is no talking down to women in *The Guardian*. Articles are written as much on the woman's point of view of national and international affairs, as on the more purely domestic issues.

'For the woman who prefers her reading not confined to the children—clothes—coiffure routine this infraction of custom is a rare quality. It is one of the reasons why *The Guardian* has more than doubled its readership in the last ten years.

'*The Guardian* respects your intelligence.'[21]

Two years later this approach had developed into:

'Fiona MacCarthy may look like a fashion model. But there are times when she writes like a sabre-toothed tiger. Particularly at the expense of pretension and plagiarism in Design.

'It is women like her, and fashion writers Phyllis Heathcote and Alison Adburgham that make the Woman's page of *The Guardian* unusually tough and informative.

'The sexes are not segregated on *The Guardian*. Defence, Health, Welfare and Travel are covered by Clare Hollingworth, Nesta Roberts and Adrienne Keith Cohen respectively. The redoubtable Lena Jeger MP writes a lively political column. And the Cookery correspondent is a man.

'Women who take an intelligent, responsible interest in their own world and the world at large will gain a great deal by reading *The Guardian*. So will men.'

Katharine Whitehorn has mapped the twentieth-century course of femininity and feminism with a shrewd accuracy which puts the crusaders in their place, and offers new hope to those millions of women beginning to feel the strain of trying to act all the different roles that society has set before them as a challenge and a duty. Miss Whitehorn notes 'a simple reaction against the perfectionism of women's mags and women's ads.'[22] This represents, she feels, the third stage of emancipation.

In stage one 'the pioneers deliberately rejected the domestic arts, played down the question of their appearance and asserted themselves in all the traditionally *un*feminine fields just to prove they could. They sometimes looked pretty grotesque doing it: front-line soldiers often do.' Stage two brought 'a second, more relaxed, attitude. The battle being more or less won—women felt—there was no reason why they should not be equally good in the home and out of it, or why one should wear hair like a bird's nest to demonstrate the egghead within.' In the third stage, 'I think we may now be coming to the realisation that perhaps all this is just *too much*, and that the ideal of the female polymath can be just as artificial as the straight either/or postures of the Pankhursts. The women who are now owning up to being bad at macaroons and unable to iron tab collars have perhaps been daunted by the ideal they have to live up to; just as the girl who is good at Latin but not games, acting but not maths, feels daunted by the headmistress's enthusiasm for the Good All-Rounder.

'They are making, maybe, a bid for the specialisation that is gaining ground everywhere else. They realise that a woman has to do a vast number of different things; but at least she needn't feel a failure if she doesn't do all of them superbly well.'

EIGHT

Battles Worth Fighting

When he married, at the age of thirty-five and not long after the first world war, a certain very successful British businessman gave his wife £20,000 to be kept in a separate account 'in case she should ever want to leave me'. During the 1939-45 war he added a further £20,000 to compensate for the fall in the value of money since the original gift was made. The marriage was extremely happy and the money was never needed, but the gesture was that of an unusually civilised man. To have money she can really call her own is the one essential mark of a free woman. Without it, she is to some extent a slave or a child and so long as millions of women, whether in Britain or anywhere else, continue to be in this position emancipation is a myth.

A human being, as Mary Stott has reminded us, is 'a creature different from the animals in being able to think, plan, and make a reasoned choice. And in a civilised society choice is dependent over and over again on the expenditure of money. Deprive a person of money of his own and you deprive him of the right of choice in a very large part of everyday life. And to deny a human being the right of choice is to humiliate and degrade him.'[1] Husbands who deny their wives money of their own 'subconsciously apprehend the truth that money means independence and that the wife with pennies in her pocket can cock a snook at him and go off on a bus to visit mamma, buy a highbrow magazine or a pop record, have a drink in a pub, or whatever she fancies. And this they cannot bear.'

Notes to this chapter are on page 179

Why a man should choose to behave like this is something which has baffled more people than Mary Stott. Why should he want to share his home with someone whom he deliberately prevents from being fully adult? Why should a woman tolerate such a situation? Why has she no legal protection in the matter? There is, of course, a very practical answer to the last question. It would be extremely difficult, if not impossible, to reach any legal definition of what would be a reasonable amount of money for each husband to allow his wife. Should it be a fixed proportion of his income? Or should some nationally agreed figure, say £2 a week, be paid to wives by their husbands as private spending money, however much or little the husband might earn? Should the husband's liability cease so long as his wife herself earns a recognised minimum sum each week? It is not a problem which the law can hope to solve, at least in any direct way. Attitudes have got to be changed, and that is a task for propaganda and persuasion. Television and women's magazines are the vehicles for this, not police stations and the courts.

If one sometimes feels pessimistic about this, it is worth remembering how much has been achieved during the past century, how many legal battles have been won, what a total serf a married woman was a hundred years ago. Her husband no longer has an automatic right to her property on marriage, she has a right to her own earnings, she can make legal contracts in her own name, she has rights over her own person, her husband's right to custody of the children has been tightly controlled, she is entitled to maintenance payments from a husband who deserts her, she can ask for a reparation order on the grounds of persistent cruelty or of her husband's imprisonment for more than two months and she can sue for divorce on exactly the same grounds as men.

She can still feel aggrieved about the unequal guardianship of children, inequalities in jury service, the inability to choose her own domicile and certain features of the 1660 Marriage Common Law. She is still treated like a child in a number of financial matters. 'Recently I went into a well-known furniture store, with the intention of ordering a bed to be paid for on hire-purchase terms. I was politely informed that I would have to bring my husband in "to do the paper-work" as I would not be allowed to make the purchase myself without a guarantor, because I am a woman.

'I asked if the situation would be the same if I told them that I was earning an independent salary. I was told that I would still need my husband to act as guarantor: I asked if my husband would need a guarantor; no, he would not. Poor Emily Davison. She died in vain.'[2]

She has every reason to feel extremely indignant about the British law on abortion, and about the male prejudices and reactionary influences which help to keep it in being. The refusal to allow women to say what shall happen to their own bodies causes great resentment and much suffering and injustice. In 1964, for instance, a much-respected young doctor, practising in Cornwall, was sent to prison for three years for performing an abortion on a woman who asked for his help. Many local people protested against the barbarism of a society and a legal system which allowed such a thing to happen. Their feelings were well summarised in a letter to *The Guardian* from Mrs Dora Russell, of Porthcurno.[3]

'Our inhuman and obsolete law against abortion has now claimed a fresh victim in one of the best and ablest medical men practising in Penzance, recently sent to prison for three years.

'It is tragic that even a skilled practitioner who comes to the help of women pregnant and desperate, is liable to disgrace and severe punishment. A great many people like myself believe that, in the main, a woman should have the right to determine when she will bear children and how many. Contraceptives are not always effective: for the most part such advice is refused to unmarried women. Yet there are certainly many pregnancies which, for one good reason or another, should be terminated.

'Dr — is held in such esteem for his skill and generosity by his patients and all who know him that a petition is being organised on his behalf. He is still young and we hope to restore him to his wife and five children and to medical practice as soon as may be possible.'

Throughout 1965 and 1966 attempts were made to get a Bill through Parliament which would bring the British abortion laws up to date, making unskilled, back-street abortion unnecessary. The Act to emerge from the emotive battle with powerful individuals who, however benevolent their reasons, do not apparently see women as twentieth-century human beings, is watered-down. With one or two improvements, it leaves the situation much as it was.

Abortion would not, of course, be the problem it is if contraceptive advice were more easily available to the people who need it most. Yet, although Britain is liberal in this respect, compared with such countries as France, Italy and Spain, there is as already noted, a strong male reluctance to concede that it is a woman's business to decide whether she has children or not and that the arrival of a reliable and aesthetically acceptable form of contraception, in the form of the pill, has made it possible to achieve a sexual morality which is not based on fear. The pill's potential as a positive contribution to relationships within marriage, with the consequent enrichment of the personalities—and therefore the value to the community—of both partners, is only slowly being understood. Gillian Reeve, among others who have studied the question, believes that the possible medical dangers from the pill have been greatly exaggerated, for a reason not difficult to discover: the attitude of certain doctors is almost certainly based on something much more radical than anxiety as to its pharmacological effects.[4] This 'something' is that 'easy and foolproof contraception represents a serious threat to the established order of society, which holds that sex in marriage is for the procreation of children and sex out of marriage is wrong. Many eminent doctors have issued dire warnings of increase in venereal disease, loose living and parental irresponsibility during the past eleven years, and will doubtless continue to do so.'[5] Worse still the pill threatens the traditional mystique of the dominant active male—passive female relationship, for a woman not doomed to perpetual parturition has time and opportunity not only actively to enjoy her sex life but also to establish other interests outside the home. 'The pill,' declared one opponent, 'affects the woman in her most important attribute—her femininity.'

This determination to maintain 'the established order of society', the belief that 'femininity' will vanish if not fettered, extends to refusing to give a woman contraceptive advice without the permission of her husband; women doctors, not surprisingly, have shown much more courage than men in disregarding this unwritten law and in being prepared to face any legal consequences. A long and illuminating correspondence in *The Guardian* in March 1966 made clear that, from a legal point of view, women are far from being free agents in what they are surely entitled to regard as an entirely personal matter.

The correspondence is worth summarising at length, since it shows how far women still have to go in a campaign which did not interest the original vote-centred suffragettes at all. It began with a letter from a woman living in Surrey whose precise complaint was as follows:

'The other day when visiting my local family planning clinic to inquire into the availability of an intra-uterine coil I was informed that this could only be fitted after I had obtained the signed permission of my husband. It seems to me outrageous that in this country, which at least pays lip-service to the equality of the sexes, such a flagrant breach of individual liberty can be allowed to arise. I should be glad to hear that the Family Planning Association will ensure that this medieval procedure will cease forthwith.'[6]

Sir Theodore Fox, on behalf of the Family Planning Association, wrote to say the clinic acted correctly. This produced two further letters. The first, from a woman in north-west London, asked: 'If, as Sir Theodore Fox suggests, the law requires a doctor who supplies a woman with an intra-uterine contraceptive to get her husband's permission first, what civil remedy, if any, would a woman have against a doctor who performed a vasectomy on her husband without consulting her?'

The second letter came from a woman doctor in Glastonbury.

'Concerning husband's consent for the fitting of an intra-uterine coil, I wrote on this subject (about all family planning, not on IUCD only) to the Medical Defence Union in 1964. They replied: "You are certainly allowed to give contraceptive advice to a wife whether or not her husband is agreeable. An adult patient is an individual with his own individual rights and the treatment or advice which you give to one partner in a marriage is, in theory, confidential even so far as the spouse is concerned." This seems perfectly clear to me and I have always followed this rule. I have worked for the FPA for years; one gets a good deal of advice from on high, which I consider, accept or reject as I think right. (As indeed I do with any advice.)'

These letters produced an up-to-date ruling from the Medical Defence Union. It ran as follows:

'In her letter (March 23) Mrs — recorded her objections to the Family Planning Association's requirement that a husband's written consent should be provided by a woman who wishes to be fitted with an intra-uterine contraceptive device. Dr Openshaw has correctly quoted our advice given in September 1964 which appears to conflict with the comments of Sir Theodore Fox in his letter on behalf of the FPA. Dr Openshaw had inquired where "contraceptive advice" could be given to a wife without the husband's consent and was given the answer which she quoted, which is still our view.

'The IUCD and "the pill", however, pose particular problems, for both these are methods of contraception which a woman can practise secretly and without her husband's knowledge. Counsel's opinion was, therefore, sought. In an exhaustive review of the legal position, Counsel expressed the opinion that a husband might have a right of action in damages against a doctor who inserted an IUCD into the wife, either without the husband's prior consent or knowing that the husband opposed his wife using any method of contraception, unless the insertion of the device was reasonably necessary in the interests of the wife's health. Counsel added that the same considerations could apply in relation to the prescribing of "the pill". The FPA therefore on the Medical Defence Union's advice warns its doctors that a husband's prior consent should always be obtained before a woman is fitted with an IUDC. Similar advice is given to members of the MDU.

'Counsel also considered Mrs —'s question and advised that the husband or the wife might have a right of action in damages against a surgeon who sterilised one spouse either without the consent or in the face of a positive prohibition by the other.'

Despite the Medical Defence Union's sop to women in the last paragraph of its letter, the outcome of this important public argument is a ruling that a woman's body is still controlled by her husband, and in this sense the feminist movement has achieved no success whatever, since this is what the century-long argument has really been about. But courageous and determined people go on trying and each year brings its little gleams of hope.

Those who have attempted to help teenagers by giving them reliable contraceptive advice, as a realistic means of avoiding unwanted pregnancies, have found themselves particularly obstructed and abused. The most frequently heard objection is that they are 'encouraging immorality', which does not appear to face the real situation. Here too it has been women doctors who have decided to snap their fingers at the backwoodsmen. In 1966, two women doctors at Sheffield raised enough money to open a clinic which specialised from the outset in giving advice and help on sexual problems to single girls, and selling contraceptives.[7] Drs Elizabeth Wilson and Jill Tattersall, both married and with families, believed that their clinic was badly needed in order to fill a gap in the services of the Family Planning Association, which decided two years earlier to help only married people.

It could usefully be noted, perhaps, that the most efficient contraception does not solve a girl's emotional problems. Men who casually sleep around with girls with whom they have no permanent relationship are guilty of profoundly anti-feminist behaviour. They usually have no understanding of the degree to which a girl becomes emotionally involved and of the extent to which her concentration on studies or career can be upset and possibly wrecked. Contraceptive advice is all very well once a stable relationship has been formed, but by itself it may cause as many problems as it solves. Too ardent a plea for its exponents can harm their own cause by over-simplification of complex issues.

In one aspect of sexuality women have been more fortunate than men. Lesbians have never been persecuted to the extent that male homosexuals have, probably because their activities are felt to be less socially damaging and to be practised by only small numbers. A new monthly magazine for lesbians, *Arena Three*, published by the Minorities Research Group, appeared in 1964. Its second issue aimed at showing that lesbianism is only a problem when society makes it so, and that it is not limited to only a few women.[8] The magazine quotes one of the few surveys carried out in which over half the women questioned 'had at some time or other experienced intense emotional relationships with other women, and that a quarter admitted that the relationship was carried to the point of overt homosexual expression.' *Arena Three* gives support to Simone de Beauvoir's view that lesbianism is a 'flight from or reaction against the inferior position of women in our culture'. It seems probable indeed that many women have been made puzzled and unhappy by feeling obliged to accept male standards of sexual enjoyment. Dr John Rowan Wilson has written well about this.[9]

'There is a constant tendency to become obsessed with orgasm. Orgasm has been spoken of as if it were a psychological necessity, without which life was hardly worth living. Spinsters have been regarded with pity, celibates with total incomprehension. The word "frustration" has come to refer to one thing, and one thing alone. This is surely to overrate the sexual act beyond all reason. To do without orgasm is, indeed, to be deprived of an important form of human satisfaction, but it is not the end of the world. Life is full of deprivations and frustrations. Men can be equally frustrated in their desire for status, independence, or physical action as they can about sex. And indeed most of them are. Frustration, in some degree or another, is a normal part of life.

'This great concern with orgasm is essentially a male preoccupation. As Pamela Hansford Johnson pointed out in a recent book, few women enjoy the sexual act unless their emotions are involved. Orgasm for its own sake means little to them, and they are not naturally promiscuous; they become so in order to hold on to men or because they have been persuaded by books written by men that it is the correct and healthy thing to do. The sexual customs of our present society are largely due to the successful imposition of male standards on women. Perhaps we need to fight for a new form of freedom for women—the freedom to say no.' For the freedom, too, perhaps, to be considered as people, not as mere sexual objects.

The nude magazines are not of course concerned with real women at all. The captions to the photographs present a philosophy in which women are no more than mindless bodies, sexual playthings. 'She has a warm, sensitive face, big beautiful eyes, silky blonde hair, and an unforgettable 38-24-36 figure.' Even the paperback edition of Simone de Beauvoir's *The Second Sex,* a highly intelligent book written to explain women as complete people, has a nude on the cover. The world of commercial nudity and strip-tease is a world in which women's values are trodden on: as J. B. Priestley has splendidly said, with particular reference to America, 'A society in which a man takes his wife for a night out and they pay extra, out of their common stock of dollars, to see another woman undressing herself is a society in which the male has completely imposed his values.'[10] After decades of striving, women have obtained no more than 'showing victories that conceal terrible defeats inflicted upon Woman herself, by the organisation and character of this society, in which she is compelled to appear not as her true self, but as the reflection of man's immature, half-childish, half-adolescent fancies and dreams. Victorious woman forms a lasting relationship with a mature man. Defeated woman strips and teases.'

Throughout the western world, women are regarded primarily as sexual beings and secondarily as human beings. As Olaf Lagercrantz, the executive editor of the Swedish newspaper *Dagens Nyheter* has said: 'The emancipation of women is just starting. It is horrible to see how throughout the western world communities are planned and built as if homes will continue to be isolated cells for evermore. In the suburban paradise among children and flowers women wait for the master-breadwinner to return.'[11] The paper edited by Mr Lagercrantz decided in 1965 to call all 'mature women' Mrs, whether they are married or not. The two Social Democratic papers *Aftonbladet* and *Stockholms Tidningen* followed suit for all women over twenty. The theory behind the change is that the Miss/Mrs distinction results in women being thought of sexually, not as people. It can be seen as an insult to women that society, which is controlled by men, distinguishes in titles between married and unmarried women, but not between married and unmarried men. Behind this the Swedes feel, is the crude convention that Miss, whatever her age, is a virgin.

The change has not been universally welcomed. Many unmarried Swedish women in their twenties are afraid that the automatic award of the prefix Mrs will make them appear older, and that this in time will make them less marriageable. No other country in Europe has yet gone as far as Sweden in this. In West Germany, however, women must no longer be identified in official documents as 'Miss', 'Mrs', or 'widow'. It is felt that such titles violate the constitutional provision that men and women are equal.

The abolition of the word for Miss, whatever the language and whatever the motive, does nothing to solve the practical problems of the unmarried woman, who so often has a harsh struggle to maintain herself and to look after a mother or other relative as well. At its easiest, the burden involves withdrawal from public life and renunciation of personal pleasures. At its worst it involves misery and privation, a non-life, which is neither dignified nor enriched by bandying around the empty title of Mrs. This form of the feminine predicament is less prevalent than it was fifty years ago, simply because a much higher proportion of women are now married, but where it occurs it is as crippling and oppressive as ever. Now and again the personal sacrifice reaches the surface for general inspection.

'Miss Mary McIntyre, a headmistress, has withdrawn as prospective Parliamentary Labour candidate for Northwich in order to nurse her widowed mother who has been taken ill. Miss McIntyre was adopted candidate in May 1962. The seat is held by a Conservative, Sir John Foster.' One does not know for certain if Miss McIntyre *had* to drop her outside prospects. She may simply have felt the family tie to be more important or satisfying. But Sir John would almost certainly not have given up his seat in order to nurse his widowed father; nor would a man find it necessary to withdraw as a Parliamentary candidate under the same circumstances. Instances such as that of Miss McIntyre represent a great social waste, as well as a serious injustice. In an attempt to improve the situation in Britain, the National Council for the Single Woman & her Dependants was founded in November 1965. Its aim is to put pressure on the Government to give these families more consideration in the social-welfare administration. Information in the Council's possession reveals a tremendous amount of strain in families consisting of a single woman with dependants, particularly when the woman has to earn and to look after the elderly person or persons. She often copes with the double task only at great cost to her own health, so that when she gets older and is alone she becomes a charge on the community. It would be cheaper, as well as kinder, for the community to do something for these people before the breakdown occurs. What is required is an increase in the Dependant

Relative allowance and/or a National Assistance allowance for care and attention. The present policy, if it can be called that, is to wait until the single woman herself becomes a complete charge on the state.

By far the biggest difficulty for the single woman is the housing shortage—the torment of every group outside the higher-income brackets. In most areas, her chances of a council house are infinitesimal; her chances of finding anything within her means—whether she lives alone or with her old parents—very small; she can almost write off her chances of being granted a mortgage. She would be much better off as a widow, when a council house, tax relief, pensions, and above all, sympathy would all open up to her. As it is many unmarried women eventually come to ask themselves in despair 'Am I doomed to a bed-sitter for the rest of my life?'

The merging of Mrs and Miss, however well-intentioned, will not produce any immediate levelling-up of female status, whatever *Dagens Nyheter* may think, so long as a majority of men insist on treating women as mindless bodies. Any woman who often travels alone knows how difficult it is on occasions to be simply a person. Apart from the inferior treatment she is almost certain to receive from porters, receptionists and waiters, everywhere she goes, in aeroplanes, trains, hotels, restaurants, press receptions and trade fairs, men, especially salesmen, will regard her as fair game. They could, if they chose, make life much easier for the woman away from home.

'They could stop their tedious nudge-and-wink routine. They could try to talk to a woman without a double entendre. Innuendo seems to be a point of honour: by themselves they may forget it, but in a crowd of colleagues they don't dare. This makes communication very complex. One's simplest comment is seized upon with roars of ribald laughter, as if every second word you'd said was bed. We can educate our women for all we're worth, give them good jobs and, maybe, eventually feminise hotels. But some of our sons, our fathers, and our grandfathers will always, I'm afraid, fight back: their sexual bravado, like Falstaff's, outlives the performance and lasts well into the grave.'[12]

The most effectively anti-feminist behaviour consists of treating women as if they were good for nothing but bed. It is this kind of patronising attitude which educated women in particular find so infuriating. In noting the evidence of the inferior role which women are still expected to tolerate, one finds oneself all the time moving between items of news which, although perhaps small in themselves, reveal a complete standstill or even regression in male attitudes. Take, for a lighter instance, the attitude of the Belgians toward shoe-cleaning. In 1964, a confession by Mrs Harold Wilson that Britain's Prime Minister dealt personally with his shoes every morning provoked acid comment in the Belgian Socialist paper *Le Peuple*.[13] The writer reproaches Mrs Wilson for not cleaning her husband's shoes, Mr Wilson for not seeing that she does it, and Anglo-Saxon wives in general for their attitude to their men. It is extremely sad, he says, that a Prime Minister should have to waste his valuable time on menial tasks like this when the fate of the Commonwealth lies in his hands. 'Is there not a reason to lack confidence in a Prime Minister who has to govern dozens of millions of souls when he has not even enough authority to ensure that his wife polishes his shoes?'

One can smile and say 'Maybe' when Dr V. A. Petrow, of British Drug Houses, tells the British Association that youth pills giving women clear skins and ample vigour long after middle-age are being perfected as a by-product of oral contraceptives, and assures the delegates that 'before long women will take one pill a day after they have reached the change of life, and this will put off the effects of senility and ageing.'[14]

One can sniff a piece of straight old-fashioned, anything-they-can-do-we-can-do-better feminism a mile off, and in most cases write it off as irrelevant to present conditions. If the football match between the Ladies of Ipswich and the Ladies of Stowmarket had to be abandoned after the referee had ordered one of the Ipswich players off the field for fighting and hair-pulling, we may feel in touch with sexual equality of a sort, but as a protest against man's superiority it strikes one as being in a minor key.[15] If one is looking for meaningful public gestures, Niki de Saint Phalle's strange household monsters, her nanas, are much to be preferred, because they have a conscious philosophy behind them.

'Being a woman today,' she has declared, 'is rather like being a Negro; you are a member of a second-class group. The world today is dominated by the white male, and I for one am getting pretty sick of that.' The nanas, strange dumpy fibreglass creations, are a token of her dissatisfaction. What they are in effect saying is 'We are bigger and warmer and more enduring than men. We are also sensitive and practical and we can rehabilitate the world. We can stop the war in Vietnam, halt the arms race, provide food for the starving and comfort for the lonely. In short, given the chance, we can clean up the monumental mess that Caucasian man has got us into.'[16] The nanas are the result of tough thinking. They are in an idiom that Mrs de Saint Phalle's contemporaries can understand and they get the public slightly off balance, which makes for vulnerability. They are universal symbols, appealing to all age-groups and all classes. They might achieve something, always provided the message is supplied with the nana, as a package deal.

There is no doubt that even well-established male vested interests are vulnerable to well-organised pressure from women. An example of this was seen early in 1968 when the vigorous campaign by wives and mothers of Hull fishermen for stronger safety measures on trawlers brought quick results. The women were almost bound to win: several trawlers had recently been lost and their crews drowned, the shipowners were unpopular figures and it was being alleged that both the owners and the skippers took great risks in the hope of large profits. Reporters toured the area picking up remarks which were pure Fleet Street gold, such as 'There's only us cares about our men. The owners sit pretty in their warm offices with their cigars,' and 'I lost my husband, a bosun, four years ago, when I had five children at school. The owners gave me

£300.'[17] One began to wonder if the year was 1968 at all.

Even so, improvements would have probably been slow in coming if fate had not presented the women with a spectacular and camera-worthy leader in the shape of the large and eloquent Mrs Lillian Bilocca—who was subsequently dismissed by her employers. Mrs Bilocca called meetings, led marches to the docks, threatened to board trawlers to stop them sailing and to smash down the office doors of the owners, 'even if it means going to gaol'. Asked by a television interviewer if she saw herself in the line of the suffragettes, Mrs Bilocca endeared herself to viewers by slapping down the man from the BBC with a large smile and three well-chosen words: 'Don't be daft.' A deputation made its way to London and was most courteously received by the President of the Board of Trade, who promised to take immediate action and did. With the help of television, the suffragettes would almost certainly have won the vote years earlier.

One of the major battles women still have to win is the fight to be allowed mental robustness. Women magistrates have got to insist on inspecting the horrifying photographs and seeing the worst obscenities spelt out. The sort of incident that occurred during the hearing of the Moors murder case at Hyde Magistrates' Court, Cheshire, undermines the dignity and status of women in public positions and has got to become obsolete. When the detective-sergeant who had taken photographs of the position and marks on the body of the murdered child had given evidence, Mr Mars-Jones, addressing Mrs Dorothy Adamson, the chairman of the magistrates, said: 'Madam, I have not asked you to look at these photographs. I think it would be better if you did not.'

There should be, at the very least, ridicule and protest and if possible in the absence of a legal injunction some self-denying vow on the part of newspapers and magazines not to publish insulting anti-feminist material of the kind in a recent *Sunday Times* advertisement for a cheap edition of two novels by Colette, *Gigi* and *Cheri*.[18] The advertisement begins, 'You can learn more about women by reading these two books than by marrying a dozen of them,' and continues: 'Let's face it, women are difficult. There are parts of every woman's heart that no one knows—not husbands, not lovers—not even sisters or mothers. Even the greatest writers . . . men of insight and sensitivity . . . have usually failed when they set out to reveal the secret corners of a woman's heart. But thank God for Colette! Not only was she one of the great authors of all times. She was *all woman*. She had no masculine affectations in either her public or private life. She lived, acted, reacted, and wrote like a woman. She cast brilliant illumination into the mysterious shadows of a woman's heart. Most heroines of literature seem lifeless and two-dimensional beside the warm, womanly sensuality of a Colette creation.'

There are times when all the struggles to escape from Victorianism seem to have led back to the starting point.

But not all women look like Colette creations, at least on the surface. In the last week of 1966 *The Sunday Times* decided that Britain was coming to the end of a Year for Women. Twenty 'firsts' were listed as evidence of this. Some of these pioneering women had achieved more than one 'first' during the year. Their activities and successes ranged over a wide field. The catalogue was as follows:

1 First woman secretary of the Institution of British Engineers and first woman to lead a trade mission to China, Mrs Dorothy Henry.
2 First person to pass the Law Society's finals with first-class honours under the new syllabus, Miss Susan Rowlands.
3 First woman executive secretary of a livery company and first woman on the Council of the Air League, Miss Gillian Mackay, a pilot.
4 First woman Minister of State for Foreign Affairs, formerly Parliamentary Under-Secretary to the Colonies, Mrs Eirene White, MP.
5 First woman to sit on the Woolsack in the House of Lords as a Deputy Speaker, Baroness Wootton of Abinger, life peeress.

6 First woman keeper appointed by the British Museum, to the National Reference Library of Science, Miss Maysie Webb.

7 First woman president of the National Association of Local Government Officers, Miss Marian Curtin.

8 First woman to win the British Gliding Championship, Mrs Anne Burns.

9 First person to fly solo 30,000 miles round the world in a single-engined aircraft in thirty-three days, Miss Sheila Scott.

10 First woman elder ordained to a kirk session in the Church of Scotland, Miss Catriona MacLean, seventeenth Laird of Ardgour.

11 First woman trainer to be granted a licence by the Stewards of the Jockey Club, Mrs Florence Nagle.

12 First woman appointed to a British National Export Council Area Committee, Mrs Elsie Lawson.

13 First woman director of the Cunard Steam Ship Company and first woman speaker at the American Bar Association dinner, Lady Tweedsmuir.

14 First woman to be appointed chairman of the Lord Chancellor's Legal Aid Advisory Committee, Baroness Emmet of Amberley.

15 First woman president of the British Association for the Advancement of Science, Dame and Professor Kathleen Lonsdale.

16 First woman chairman of the Metropolitan Water Board, Dame Florence Cayford.

17 First woman to score top marks at the final examination held by the Institute of Quantity Surveyors, Mrs Janet Brown.

18 First woman chairman of the Conservative Political Centre, National Advisory Committee, Dame Margaret Shepherd.

19 First woman alderman to be elected to the City of London's Court of Common Council in over seven centuries, Lady Mary Donaldson.

20 First woman president of a Junior Chamber of Commerce, Miss Angela Hooper of Southampton.

Probably an assiduous journalist could have assembled just as impressive a collection of 'firsts' for 1965 or 1967. The significance of the list, however, is that these twenty 'firsts' represent twenty long-drawn-out battles won; they are symbols of a real change in the atmosphere. In 1916 there would not have been a woman president of the British Association or for that matter a woman trainer with a Jockey Club licence.

Nowadays newspapers and magazines are always on the look-out for Women Who Do Things. Articles about them appear to interest readers of both sexes, especially when the achievement has a certain rarity value, as in the case of a woman quantity-surveyor or judge. What is really wanted, to provide encouragement and raise morale, is an annual handbook, with plenty of potted biographies. It might be called *What British Women Have Done In 1968* or whatever the year might be and it would range over as wide a field as possible. Some women would appear only once, others would justify their inclusion year after year.

The cumulative effect of each issue would be considerable. The subjects would include people like Mrs Marie Louise Cohen, of Brighton, aged thirty-one and partner in a cosmetics firm. In September 1967 Mrs Cohen won a High Court action against the British Institute of Management allowing her to continue to seek election to its council. At that time the council had fifty-eight members, all men, but in the twenty years since its foundation two women seem to have been on it. BIM fought hard to keep Mrs Cohen out, claiming that her ballot paper had not gone out in time because it had not been satisfied about what precise description to put on it, but the Judge said Mrs Cohen had been perfectly properly nominated and the Institute had to think again. Mrs Cohen would appear to have been a most suitable candidate for election, with an MA degree in industrial organisation and working for a PhD on the effectiveness of the various kinds of management studies.

Another woman to qualify would be Miss Catherine Avent, Director of the Careers Advisory Service, which is part of the London Youth Employment Service and advises school-leavers on professional careers. One of the highest-paid women public servants, she read English at Oxford, served in the WRNS, and is now in her mid-forties. She admits to being fond of writing and talking and committees, and disliking domesticity. 'I dislike babies,' she is reported to have said. 'I don't want to cuddle them. It's an insult to me to think humans are so dependent.'

She is well aware of the personal problems that higher education can create for women. 'No one wants to marry a girl who's had more education than himself. Going to university automatically narrows the field. But I wish I knew the answer to what girls' education should be. It's a great pity that there seems to be a need for a girl to disguise her education. It shouldn't matter as long as we're not aggressive about it.'

The career of Miss Ann Chambers of Sidmouth, Devon, might surprise and stimulate some of the readers of our suggested handbook. In June 1965, at the age of twenty-two, she became the first woman in Britain to qualify as a naval architect. She had been awarded a Diploma in Naval Architecture after completing a three-year course at Sunderland Technical College, the only college willing to take her. She was the only woman student in an engineering faculty of 400 men and finished up in the top six.

Mrs Avril Fox would certainly deserve mention as chairman of the Cosmo Group which opposes Mrs Mary Whitehouse's campaign to 'clean up' BBC programmes. Mrs Fox, who is forty-nine, divorced, lives in Harlow and was formerly a member of the Communist party. She agrees with Simone de Beauvoir that women are products of their environment in so far as the qualities that men like to think of as being masculine are bred out of them, to the disadvantage both of themselves and of society. She regrets that western society has not so far recognised that the time of life normally thought of as decline is, on the contrary, a time of fruition. 'I think,' she has said, 'that it would help women a lot in their attitude towards the ties of marriage if they felt that when their children had grown up, both spouses could consider starting a new life —perhaps with different partners, partners of the same sex, or even no partners at all. But I fear that we're a long way from such mature considerations.'

There would be a good selection of such formidably energetic and well-organised women as Dorothy Hodgkin, winner of the Nobel Prize for Chemistry, who brought up three children with great success, kept herself in the forefront of her subject and divided her life between Oxford, where her own work was, and Accra, where her husband was Director of the Institute for African Studies.

Another dynamo is Anne Shaw, never projected to the general public as she should have been, although she is well-known within her own specialist field of management consultancy. When her second child was only two months old, she joined the Ministry of Aircraft Production and was appointed to the Production Efficiency Board, to report on the use of labour in the aircraft industry. When her third child was born three years later, she started her own firm of management consultants, the Anne Shaw Organisation. In 1964 she formed a second company to advise on electronic data processing and the use of computers. She tried to solve her work-and-family problem by introducing work-study into her own home. Afterwards she came to feel that this kind of struggle wasn't worth the effort and the exhaustion; for a professional woman who intends to continue with her career, the first essential, she believes, is to earn enough to be able to pay for efficient, reliable domestic help.

She had a tough academic education, reading first mathematics and then psychology and social science at Edinburgh, and is strongly opposed to Sir John Newsom's campaign to give girls a separate and different education from boys. The idea of sexual difference in ability is, she thinks, a dangerous myth, and needs to be fought. Anne Shaw belongs to a generation which had to struggle against prejudice in order to be able to study and work in a traditionally male field. The prospect of a reversion to sex distinction in education seems to her, and to most other professional women of her generation, like a return to the Dark Ages. She is equally hostile towards trained women taking inferior jobs, merely because such jobs are to be had without difficulty. Computer programming she thinks of as an inferior job which women mathematics graduates would do well to avoid. 'They shouldn't do it,' she says. 'For women it's a dead end.'

And if dead ends are wrong for men, they are equally wrong for women. The emphasis is on 'equally'. The time has surely come to drop the pointless concept of a war between the sexes. Forty years ago, when the dust of the suffragette battles was still in the air, Virginia Woolf took stock of the position: 'All this pitting of sex against sex, of quality against quality; all this claiming of superiority and imputing of inferiority, belong to the private-school stage of human existence where there are "sides", and it is necessary for one side to beat another side, and of the utmost importance to walk up to a platform and receive from the hands of the Headmaster himself a highly ornamental pot. As people mature they cease to believe in sides or in Headmasters or in highly ornamental pots.'[19]

Very recently, Katharine Whitehorn has demanded, in *The Observer*, the same truce, the same end to people shouting for their own side, instead of trying to see the rights and wrongs of the individual case, the same abolition of standard norms to which men and women are expected to conform. 'Whether you like it or not, a society of a million differences is what we've actually got. It's taken some time to work back to the notion that they are also different from one another.

'As a feminine trade unionist, I've fought the sex war long and hard. I'm now prepared to call a cease-fire in the interests of a negotiated peace.'[20] The main difficulty may be to know which of the million different kinds of men and which of the million kinds of women are to be the negotiators.

Notes

INTRODUCTION
(Pages 7-12)

1 *Votes for Women* (1957), p 15
2 *Lady into Woman* (1953), p 4
3 In accordance with the law of 31 July 1920, adopted by an all-male Parliament with the aim of building up the French population to its pre-war level. Primarily aimed at the suppression of abortion, it was passed in such a hurry that contraception was confused with abortion.
4 Reported in *Le Nouvel Observateur*, 22 April 1965
5 For a discussion of this, see *New Society*, 1 April 1965
6 The Bill presented to Parliament in January 1968 to reform the British divorce law attempted to establish only one ground on which a petition for divorce might be presented, the irretrievable breakdown of the marriage.
7 *Financial Times*, 24 November 1965. The Equal Employment Opportunity Commission has recently been under pressure from a new feminist organisation, NOW (National Organisation for Women). NOW has produced a bill of rights for women, for which it is intended to campaign during the 1968 Presidential Election campaign. The aim is full sexual equality, and the organisation's president is Betty Friedan, author of *The Feminine Mystique.*
8 9 January 1965. cf another *Times* obituary, 11 December 1963, of 'Mrs Margaret Fisher Prout, woman painter of individual talent'. On the other hand *The Times* published on 5 June 1968 a Woman's Page article about Bridget Riley and Sandra Blow, 'painters who have achieved world recognition', which asked 'What is the quality of a woman's vision?'
9 *Times*, 15 July 1966.

CHAPTER ONE

The Roots of Anti-Feminism (pages 13-36)

1 A version of this famous incident is to be found in Pamela Brookes, *Women at Westminster*, p 22. 'Winston Churchill, who had often been her guest, was one who ignored her. One day she challenged him about this and he replied that he found a woman's intrusion into the House of Commons as embarrassing as if she had burst upon him in his bathroom when he had nothing to defend himself with but a sponge. "Nonsense, Winston," she retorted, "you are not good-looking enough to have fears of this sort." '

2 On this point, Smith took a more liberal view than either Huxley or Darwin. Huxley had written, 'In every excellent character, whether mental or physical, the average woman is inferior to the average man, in the sense of having that character less in quantity and lower in quality . . . Even in physical beauty man is superior.' In Darwin's view: 'It is generally admitted that with women the powers of intuition or rapid perception, and perhaps of imitation, are more strongly marked than in man, but some at least of these faculties are characteristic of the lower races, and therefore of a past and lower state of civilisation.'

In his often reprinted book, *The Psychology of Sex* (1949), a modern psychiatrist, Dr Oswald Schwarz, reinforces the belief that there are ineradicable mental differences between men and women. 'However great the social plasticity of human nature may be, it cannot be denied that the male personality radically differs from the female. It is easy to see that it must be so, because each sex has an existence radically different from the other.' (Penguin edition, pp 119-20)

See also Simone de Beauvoir, *Force of Circumstance*. 'I had never had any feeling of inferiority, no one had ever said to me: "You think that way because you're a woman", my femininity had never been irksome to me in any way. "For me," I said to Sartre, "you might almost say it just hasn't counted." "All the same, you weren't brought up in the same way as a boy would have been, you should look into it further." I looked, and it was a revelation, this world was a masculine world, my childhood had been nourished by myths forged by men, and I hadn't reacted to them in at all the same way I should have done if I had been a boy.' (Penguin edition, p 103)

3 The Reform Act of 1884 had given every male householder the vote. Many of them were totally illiterate.

4 The same point had been made much earlier by Herbert Spencer. On this see Fulford, *Votes for Women*, p 78: 'Herbert Spencer, over a cup of tea with Lady Amberley, told her that unless women could fight they should not vote.'

5 In *Lady into Woman* (1953). But she ignores one powerful attraction that war may have for many women. When their husbands are no longer there to be relied on day by day, they are left with responsibility for their own lives, and they find this enjoyable. As Simone de Beauvoir has said: 'Women left to their own resources for a time, though they may sincerely regret their husbands' absence, are often surprised and pleased to discover that in such circumstances they have unsuspected possibilities, they take charge, bring up children, make decisions, carry on without help. They find it irksome when the return of their men dooms them again to incompetence.' (*The Second Sex*. Four Square edition, pp 202-3)

6 *Western Gazette*, 23 February 1968

7 *Guardian*, 14 August 1967

8 *The Princess*

9 *A Room of One's Own*, p 148. In a review of the Garbo film *Queen Christina*, recently revived, Penelope Gilliatt noted (*Observer*, 11 August 1963) that Garbo 'always seems miles beyond the boundaries of sex, equally and pityingly remote from the men who are in love with her and the women who are vying with her'. Elizabeth Taylor, she thinks, is for this reason an actress of an altogether lesser order. 'The crucial thing missing in Elizabeth Taylor's *Cleopatra* is a streak of masculinity. The ideal now in all Hollywood films is a kind of pedigree sexuality; pure-bred virile man, pure-bred female woman: it doesn't seem very realistic psychologically, and it certainly isn't helpful dramatically. To play the big parts actors and actresses have always needed a bit of the other gender in their veins; to feel, in fact, sexual mongrels.'

10 ibid, p 149

11 'The American Woman', in *Journey Down a Rainbow* (1955). Included in *The World of J. B. Priestley*, p 146

12 ibid, p 147

13 See Edna Ferber, *A Kind of Magic*.
'For me there is no greater bore than a 100-per-cent male or female. Confronted by a massive two-fisted, barrel-chested he-man, or a fluttering itsy-bitsy, all-tendril female, I run from their irksome company. The men and women I prize are a happy blend of male and female characteristics. A man who is

masculine with a definitely female streak of perception, intuition and tenderness is a whole man; he is an interesting man, a gay companion, a complete lover. A woman who possesses a sufficient strain of masculinity to make her thoughtful, decisive, worldly in the best meaning of the word; fair; self-reliant; companionable—this is a whole woman. The feminine in the man is the sugar in the whisky. The masculine in the woman is the yeast in the bread. Without these ingredients the result is flat, without tang or flavour.'

14 Inger Becker, 'Men in need of protection', *New Society*, 7 September 1967

15 See *Le Nouvel Observateur*, 25 March 1965

16 *Lady into Woman* (1953), p 23

17 Myron Brenton, *The American Male*, 1967, pp 225-6

18 Mary McCarthy, *Vietnam*, 1967, p 93

19 Donald Duncan, *The New Legions*, 1967, pp 94, 108, 248

20 Anglo-American Productivity Council, *Internal Combustion Engines Productivity Team Report*, 1949, p 7

21 *The Better Half—The Emancipation of the American Woman*, 1966, p 351

22 *Black Nationalism* (Penguin, 1966, p 86)

CHAPTER TWO
The Education of Women (pages 37-53)

1 9 September 1966
2 *Observer*, 6 September 1964
3 13 September 1964
4 Dr Ollerenshaw avoids controversy and confines herself almost entirely to statistics and description, even over such matters as the curriculum and boarding schools, where public argument abounds. In *Locked-up Daughters*, Felicia Lamb and Helen Pickthorn grapple with the rights and wrongs of boarding schools, but their information seems strangely partial and incomplete.
5 *Observer*, 27 October 1964
6 On this see an interesting article by George Taylor, Chief Education Officer for Leeds, in *The Guardian*, 14 July 1964
7 *A Career for Women in Industry*, by Nancy Seear, Veronica Roberts and John Brock (1964). Discussed in *The Times Educational Supplement*, 18 September 1964, under the heading 'Is Science Unfeminine?' Miss Margaret Higgison, headmistress of Bolton School, has said, in *The Guardian*, 18 March 1968: 'If we want more women scientists we ought to reverse the present trend towards co-education.'
8 4 September 1964
9 See *Guardian*, 22 February 1966
10 15 April 1964
11 3 March 1966
12 ibid
13 Letter to *The Times*, 24 May 1966, referring to an article of 19 May, suggesting that mixed colleges were desirable.
14 *Observer*, 27 May 1956
15 *Where*, June 1967

CHAPTER THREE
Women in Employment (pages 54-76)

1 *Ministry of Labour Gazette*, June 1964
2 August 1966
3 15 March 1962
4 20 March 1962
5 'On Equal Terms,' 14 September 1959
6 22 March 1962
7 *Observer*, 8 May 1966, in an interview with Kenneth Harris
8 *Spectator*, 11 November 1966
9 *Economist*, 19 August 1964
10 *Guardian*, 3 February 1967
11 *Sunday Times*, 15 January 1967. *The Guardian*, 8 February 1968, published a long list of firms willing to recruit and train married women graduates who wished to return to work when their children were old enough.
12 *Times*, 31 May 1967
13 *Times Review of Industry*, November 1963
14 29 August 1964, in a review of *A Career for Women in Industry*. The British Association of Women Executives announced the formation in May 1968 of a Careers Advisory Service for Girls in Industry.
15 For evidence of this, see *Women Executives, their Training and Careers* (London Chamber of Commerce, 1966)
16 Women teachers do of course receive equal pay. A proposal to write equal pay into the 1944 Education Act was defeated as a result of the personal intervention of Winston Churchill, but it was achieved in stages during the 1950s.
17 *Times*, 24 March 1967. A pilot study of the cost of equal pay for work of equal value is now, January 1968, being conducted jointly by the TUC and the CBI.
18 *Times*, 5 July 1967. One Government department has implemented the principle of equal pay for its weekly-paid staff. Prison officers, whether men or women, receive £14 0s 0d—£19 8s 0d, together with accommodation. The reason for the women getting a man's wage is partly that the two sexes obviously do exactly the same work and partly that few women want to become prison officers.

The General & Municipal Workers' Union has taken the first real step, among British trade unions, toward equal pay for its women workers. From the spring of 1968 its negotiators have been told to press for equal monetary increases for men and women in any wage bargaining. The union recognises that higher increases for women than for men, gradually closing the gap, would be the ideal approach, but under present conditions to reduce the percentage differential is seen as a practical first line of attack.

On the political front, Mrs Joyce Butler, Labour MP for Wood Green, has pressed (*The Times*, 19 February 1968) for a Sex Discrimination Board to help women who feel they have been discriminated against, at work or elsewhere.

19 *Guardian*, 4 December 1967

20 Published September 1967

21 26 January 1967

CHAPTER FOUR
Married Women Working (pages 77-97)

1 *Lady into Woman* (1953), p 181
2 14 May 1965
3 *Character*, 1887
4 Pearl Jephcott and others, *Married Women Working* (1962), p 125. A short interim report of this study was published by HMSO as *Woman, Wife and Worker* (1960). See also E. Dahlström (editor), *The Changing Roles of Men and Women* (1967) and Alva Myrdal and Viola Klein, *Women's Two Roles* (1968—revised edition).
5 14 October 1965
6 *Married Women Working*, pp 22-3
7 Judith Hubbard, *Wives who went to College* (1957)
8 *Married Women Working*, p 91
9 *Financial Times*, 3 June 1964
10 This arrangement would probably suit middle-class arrangements less well. Most middle-class wives look on the evening as a period of activity and entertainment, even when their children are young and however hard a day their husbands may have had. Hannah Gavron reports in *The Captive Wife* (1966) that only 4 per cent of the middle-class wives she interviewed said that they never went out in the evenings, compared with 44 per cent of the working-class. The determination of middle-class wives to emerge in the evenings may be a powerful, if carefully hidden, source of anti-feminism among their husbands, whose yearning for rest in the evenings is unlikely to be less than that found among working-class husbands.
11 *The Second Sex* (Four Square Books), p 212. A survey of working wives carried out in 1963 in Detroit, Chicago and Washington by Susan R. Orden and Norman M. Bradburn, published by the National Opinion Research Center, University of Chicago, in 1968 as *Working Wives and Married Happiness*, showed that domestic tension was slight when wives worked from choice, considerable when they took jobs from economic necessity.
12 ibid, p 216
13 ibid, p 234
14 *New Society*, 20 November 1966
15 13 June 1964
16 *Times*, 15 November 1963
17 *The Second Sex*, pp 189-90

18 Speaking at a conference at Keele University. Reported in *The Guardian*, 5 April 1965

19 4 October 1965

20 *Guardian*, 31 October 1964

21 Jessie Barnard, *Academic Women* (Penn State University Press, 1965)

22 6 June 1966

23 12 April 1965

24 See, for instance, the different viewpoints of Fiona MacCarthy's pamphlet (Conservative Political Centre, 1966) and the Young Fabians' pamphlet, published in the same year.

25 For a description of the aims and methods of the course, see *New Society*, 15 October 1964

26 *Times*, 26 June 1964. A similarly run organisation is Freelance Work for Women, established by Mrs Joan Wilkins in 1963. It has an office headquarters in Camden Town, London, and sells the skills of 5,000 women.

27 *Guardian*, 11 November 1964

28 Among its other activities the centre publishes *Comeback*, a guide for educated women returning to work.

29 Katharine Whitehorn, *Observer*, 13 September 1964

CHAPTER FIVE
The Mark 2 Wife (pages 98-108)

1 A shortened version of this chapter was broadcast in *Woman's Hour* on 6 March 1967, and produced a considerable and illuminating correspondence from listeners. The letters were mainly hostile, but often worried as well.

2 *Guardian*, 24 March 1965. It is not perhaps generally known that there is an order of women Freemasons, founded in 1908. Its headquarters are at 27 Pembridge Gardens, London W.

3 On women and Freemasonry, see James Dewar, *The Unlocked Secret*, pp 77-8

4 ibid, p 78

5 ibid

6 ibid

7 *The Guardian*, 14 February 1968, reported that the practice of interviewing the wives of applicants for jobs had been rejected out of hand at a business seminar in Manchester. Mr H. E. Roff, managing director of a management selection firm, commented: 'It is quite enough to know what a man will be like in the board-room, without trying to assess what he is like in the bedroom.' In a report by J. M. and R. E. Pahl, published by the Graduate Appointments Register in 1968, on a group of eighty-six industrial managers and their wives, there is strong evidence that wives have much influence on their husbands' careers, especially in the choice of a company and a neighbourhood.

8 *Evening Standard*, 15 December 1966. It could reasonably be objected on the other hand that there is already far too much interference by public bodies in people's private lives—too many of such impertinencies as a judge forbidding Edna O'Brien to allow her children to read her books. A less suspect approach is that pioneered early in 1967 by Luton Methodist Industrial College. The college has arranged courses for wives of executives to teach them what management is about and to show them the kind of problems their husbands have to face every day in the course of their jobs.

CHAPTER SIX

Women and Public Life (pages 109-130)

1 Richard Rose, 'The Women's Vote', *Times*, 21 March 1966
2 *Guardian*, 13 October 1964
3 *Financial Times*, 9 June 1964
4 Of the eighteen Labour women elected in 1964, six became ministers, with one in the cabinet.
5 *Times*, 14 March 1966, supports this view
6 *Observer*, 4 February 1968
7 21 October 1964
8 *Guardian*, 19 December 1964
9 1 January 1965
10 *Times*, 29 March 1965
11 23 May 1965
12 *Times*, 12 November 1963. The *Daily Telegraph*, 16 February 1968, reported that three women and a man who objected to the renewal of the licence of a public house in Hull, on the ground that it refused to admit women and 'queers' to its bars, lost their case.
13 26 February 1965
14 25 May 1966
15 17 June 1964. Miss Cann, a solicitor, was forty-eight at the time of her appointment. She is married to Mr Carl Johnson, Labour MP for South Lewisham.
16 19 August 1965. Referred to in *The Times* of the following day
17 *Times*, 14 November 1967
18 *Times*, 17 November 1967
19 *Sun*, 15 November 1967
20 Reported in *The Times*, 23 March 1966
21 *Times*, 5 April 1966
22 4 May 1964
23 *Times*, 6 May 1964
24 *Times*, 7 May 1964
25 See a letter protesting against this, *Times*, 2 May 1964
26 *Times*, 30 April 1965
27 *Guardian*, 16 October 1964
28 *Guardian*, 12 August 1967
29 *Guardian*, 22 August 1967
30 *New Statesman*, 8 December 1967
31 On this see Edmund Penning-Rowsell, 'Women and Wine', *New Statesman*, 8 December 1967
32 *Financial Times*, 2 December 1964
33 *Times*, 29 July 1966

CHAPTER SEVEN
The Femininity Problem (pages 131-144)

1 See, for instance, the television critic of *The Times Educational Supplement*, 24 July 1964, who felt women to be well suited to television interviewing, 'for their subtlety and powers of divination are the natural endowment of biographers, as Elizabeth Jane Howard lately demonstrated in her astute portrait of Evelyn Waugh'.
2 *Glasgow Evening Citizen*, 28 September 1967. In a syndicated article by Milton Shulman.
3 *Times*, 2 August 1966
4 In *Thunderball*. Mr L. P. Hartley, on the other hand, suggests that only women should be allowed to drive, since their safety record is so much better. 'They do not have to prove their womanhood by murder.' (*Guardian*, 14 December 1967)
5 Elizabeth Good in *The Sunday Times*, 28 September 1964
6 *Sunday Times*, 16 January 1966
7 Miss Ann Lawson-Dick. Letter to the author, 23 June 1967
8 Reported in *The Times*, 12 November 1962
9 *Sun*, 8 December 1964. One can contrast Dr Goodheart's point of view with that of Miss Carol White, star of the film, *Poor Cow*. Speculating on the men she sees passing her pub terrace, she produces an improvised dialogue, on which she comments (*Sunday Times*, 3 December 1967), 'I mean, it's how all women go on when they look at men. They fancy them just as much as men fancy women. It's perfectly natural. Why should it be one-sided?'
10 *New Scientist*, 3 September 1964. In February 1968 Mary Quant introduced see-through blouses to be worn without bras.
11 *A Room of One's Own*, p 157
12 ibid, p 112
13 *New Statesman*, 14 December 1966
14 *Spectator*, 4 February 1966
15 *Times*, 26 July 1966
16 *New Society*, 3 December 1964. Article by W. D. McClelland.
17 ibid
18 *Sunday Telegraph*, 10 March 1967
19 13 April 1967
20 ibid
21 12 December 1963
22 *Observer*, 4 April 1965

CHAPTER EIGHT
Battles Worth Fighting (pages 145-165)

1 *Guardian*, 9 March 1964
2 *Guardian*, 3 February 1967
3 11 August 1964
4 *Guardian*, 21 August 1967
5 See Alex Comfort, *The Anxiety Makers* (1966)
6 23 March 1966
7 Reported in *The Guardian*, 31 August 1966. *The Guardian*, 12 February 1968, quoted student health reports to show that one unmarried woman student in every ten becomes pregnant during her three years at a British university. Of these pregnancies, one-third are terminated by abortion. Most Student Health Centres now issue the pill to women students, although a number prefer not to publicise the fact.
8 June 1964
9 *Spectator*, 5 May 1965
10 *The World of J. B. Priestley*, pp 156-7
11 *Guardian*, 26 October 1965
12 Fiona MacCarthy, *Guardian*, 10 August 1964
13 11 December 1964
14 *Times*, 2 September 1964
15 *Guardian*, 7 October 1964. Dr Norman Inlah, a Birmingham psychiatrist, has said that football 'is strictly masculine entertainment' (*Daily Telegraph*, 1 October 1967)
16 *Sunday Times*, 26 November 1967
17 *Sunday Times*, 3 February 1968
18 26 November 1967
19 *A Room of One's Own*, pp 159-60
20 *Observer*, 18 February 1968

Acknowledgments

The people who have helped me most are probably not aware that they have helped me at all, but I should none the less like to give them some form of public thanks. I am particularly grateful to three editors of *Woman's Hour*, Miss Joanna Scott-Moncrieff, Miss Madge Hart and Miss Monica Sims, whose encouragement and tough-mindedness have been an invaluable discipline for me. So too have the many conversations I have had over the years with two very experienced Bristol journalists, Mrs Barbara Buchanan and Mrs Daphne Hubbard.

I am a devotee of the writings of Miss Katharine Whitehorn, whom I have met only once. Her stimulating brand of common sense has done a great deal to weaken national prejudice and to build up a more reasonable relationship between the sexes.

I have tested out theories and collected evidence at hundreds of all-male and all-female meetings; I owe the members of these audiences a great debt of gratitude.

A special debt is owed to Mrs Pamela Thomas, with whom I have spent hours in creative argument, and who succeeded in persuading me to present many of my conclusions in a calmer and more sensible manner than I should otherwise have done.

Index

Index

Index